EPHESUS

Christa Sobel

HİTİT COLOR
KARTPOSTAL SANAYİ TİCARET VE PAZARLAMA LİMİTED ŞİRKETİ
Cağaloğlu yokuşu, Çele Han No.39 İstanbul Tel: 526 56 51 Fax: 520 78 49

Photographs: Hitit Color Photo Archive
Art Selection And Design: Melih Öndün
Illustration: Melek Öndün
Typesitting: Patrol Ajans

HİTİT COLOR 1992 - İstanbul

Cover: Head of Lysimachos, 3 rd. c. B.C.

ISBN 975-7487-07-4

CONTENTS

THE ESTABLISHMENT

The Hitite sources of the 14th century B.C. mention the Ahavia Kingdom and the important city Apasas of this kingdom. It is know that the Ahivia kingdom had been established around the Miletos region. The closeness of Miletos to Ephesus and the resemblance of Apasas with Efes, Ephesus or Ephesos suggests that the former name of Ephesus was Apasas. The most ancient findings in Ephesus are the Miceanean era, tomb gifts (cups) dated back to the 13-14 centuries B.C. Having not found any Micean living centers during the excavations during the last century-might indicate that Apasas had commercial relations with Micea.

According to the antiquity authors Strabon (1. cent. B.C.) and Pausanias (2nd cent. A.D.) Ephesus was founded by the Amazons. Strabon also says that Ephesus was the name of an Amazonian Queen. The fact that there was no unity among the people living in West Anatolia, was a reason for hellenic people who were speaking Aiolis, Ionic and Doric dialects, to immigrate to those regions and build colonies there. And again because these people created a religious-ritualistic unity, names such as Ionia and Aiolis were given to the coasts. In the Ionian region, where Ephesus was situated, too, were 12 cities. These were Miletos, Myus, Priene, Colophon, Lebedos, Teos, Clozomenai, Phokaia, Erythrai, Samos and Chios. The representatives of these Ionian cities would gather in a place called Panionion. The Panionion which was on the Mykale peninsula and to the south of Kuşadası, and which is now within the limits of the Güzelçamlı village, was a place where every year half-religious rituals were made

The colonization in Ephesus was completed in the 10th century B.C. Strabon and Pausanias tell us the story of the foundation of Ephesus as follows "The Athenian King Kodros'es son Androklos and his friends who wanted to immigrate to the West Anatolian Coasts asked the Apollonian Oracle where to build the new city. The Oracle tells them that a fish and a wild boar would show them the place. After a long journey they arrived at the Krystos Coast. There while frying the fish they had caught, one of the fish jumped out of the pan and set a fire by burning the dry grass around. A wild boar that had been lingering in the bushes around ran awey with fright. Androclos who had seen it chased it with his horse and shot it on a small hill by Koressos. Believing that the prophecy of the Oracle had come true they decided to build the city there.

Androclos who is considered as the ktistes (mythological founder) of Ephesus, makes good relations with the natives Carians and Lelegians. These relations are strengthened by the resemblance of the characteristics of the Mother Goddess Kybele of the Anatolians with those of the Goddess Artemis of the newcomers. When Androclos is killed in a war he is buried in Smyrna and a heroon is built on

Androclos Running after Wild Boar

his tomb. According to Strabon, Smyrna was the name of the open area in front of the Magnesia Gate. The residents later deserted Ephesus and founded the city Smyrna (Izmir). The 9th and 8th centuries B.C. of ephesus are dark, just as all other west Anatolian cities. It is supposed that Ephesus was a small city ruled by the children of Androclos.

In the 7th century B.C. Ephesus was attacked by the Kimmer tribe, like the other, onian cities were. The Kimmer who invaded the region in a fury did not stay long. They left after destroying the Artemis Temple. After the Kimmer invasions Ephesus again collected itself and gained a lot of fame in science, technology and wealth because of the Artemis Temple, among the neighboring cities. In the 6th cent. B.C. the Lydians became a very powerful state, especially through its capital Sardes and they attacked phesus. The citizens of Ephesus did not take the attack of the Lydian king Kroisos too seriously because they believed that thier Goddess Artemis would protect them. But things did not turn out as they expected and the Lydians entered Ephesus. Kroisos treated them well and he contributed to the Artemis Temple which was being built. According to Strabon he gives Columnea Caelata (engraved columns) which had his name on them. The column on which his name was engraved and other precious gifts made of ivory and gold, were found during the first excavations and taken to the British Museum. Croisos also forced the people to live in the newly founded block sites around the Temple. So the citizens deserted Cresos which they had inhabited for 400 years, and started to live by the famous Temple. The alluvions carried by the river Cystros covered the city with slam. Croisos after Ephesus included other Ioninan cities under his reign. Cyros who took the lead in Persia and tried to take advantage of the fights in Persia started for Cappadocia. But there he helped the Cappadokians instead of fiht them. The winner of the fight is not clear. Croisos gave his hired men leave until spring, the time when he planned for a new attack. But Cyros and his strong army suddenly apperade in front of Sardes. The Lydians had to surrender. Croisos fell a prisoner. According to Heredot, Cyros sent messengers to Ionian cities before he attacked Lydia, in order to ask them to rebel against Croisos, and take his side during the war. But except for Miletos no other city accepted this. After the fall of Sardes the Ionian and Aiolos cities sent representatives declaring that they were willing to be committed under the same conditions set by Croisos. But they could not prevent a persian attack. The famous persian commander Harpagos invaded all of West Anatolia starting from Phokaia (Foça) in 546 B.C.

The Persians by unifying Ionia, Aiolis, Caria, Likia, Pamphilla and South Lydia founded the Ionian Satrap which they called Yauna and made Sardes its capital. During the persian reign Ephesus was free with its inner affairs and it continued its commerçial relations. The Ionian Satrap paid Persia 400 Talents in silver as tax. The Persians took soldiers from Ephesus whenever neccessary and used the Harbor of Ephesus as a base. The tax taken by the Persians was not lifted after Cyros, on the contraray it was increased during the reigns of Kymbses and Dareios. This was a situation which made people long even for tyranny again.

Remains of Artemis Temple

THE IONIAN REVOLT

In the year 500 B.C. Aristrastos who was the tyran of Miletos, the richest and biggest city of Ionia, convinced the Satrap of Sardes, Artafarnes, to attack the Nacsos island. This attack which lasted for four months, brought the persian army no success and they had to retreat. Aristagoras who felt that his position was becoming somewhat shaky, provocated Miletos against the Persians. Plus he presented himself as the savior of the people who were complaining of high taxes and so he made other Ionian cities rebel against Persia The rebellions gathered at Ephesus and following the Cystros Coast for three days they arrived at Sardes. They took the city without any fight. Only the Satrap Arthraphenes could defend himself by withdrawing into the inner fortress. One of the rebellions set a house on fire and because the tops of the houses were made of bamboo the fire spread very quickly and burned down the whole city. The Kybele Temple also burned down in this fire. This was then used by the persians as an excuse when they burned down the temples of the Greek. When the rebellions found out that a strong persian army was coming towards them they started to flee back. The persian army reached Ephesus by following the Ionians and there they defeated the Ionian forces. In this war which is called the "Ephesus Battle" most of the Ionian soldiers were killed. Nevertheless, the revolt grew and spread all over the Aegean Islands.

The Ionian revolt came to an end in 494 B.C. when the Ionian navy was defeated by the Persians near the Lade Island. The Persians first burned down Miletos. They took some of its inhabitants as slaves to Persia and other places. Then they again attacked Ionian cities and plundered them. The Ionian revolt did as much harm to the people of Chios as it did to the citizens of Miletos. The Chiosians whose ships were sunken and who were chased by the Persians, came to the Mykele coast and put their ships ashore. They walked night and day until they came near Ephesus. The citizens of Ephesus were at that time celebrating the Termophoria holiday, in which only married women could participate. When they saw the armed Chiosians they thought that these were bandits who came to take away the women and so they slained all of the Chiosians.

In 479 B.C. the persian commander Mardonius, after invading central Greece and Attica again, was defeated and killed in Plataia. Just after this Spartacians set up a surprise attack on the persian navy and burned down the whole fleet. After this victory against the Persians, the ionian cities again revolted in order to kick the Persians out of Anatolia just as they had been kicked out of Greece. They joined the 'Athens-Delos SeaUnion' which was established by the leadership of Sparta and Athens.. According to Tukidites and Aristo, Ephesus paid 7.5 talens in 453 B.C. and 6 talens in 444 and 7.5 talens in 436 as subscription fee. If it should be considered that the amount of fee was taken with respect to its finanacial power then it can be concluded that Ephesus was one of the wealthier cities.

During the Peleponesian Wars, Ephesus took first Athen's side and then Sparta's. In the year 409 B.C. the Athenian commander Thrasyllus, whose fleet consisted of 50 ships, attacked an plundered Plgela which is to the south of Ephesus..Later he attacked Colophonn and Metropolis which are to the south of Ephnesus and the plundered the villages there.

The Persian regional commander Stages attacked the Athenians but he could not keep them from reatreating to another place called Notion. The Ionian Satrap Tissaphernes asked all the Ionian cities to defend the Artemis Temple against a possible attack of Thrasyllos. The Athenians lost the fights which took place around the city of Ephesus.

ALEXANDER THE GREAT İN EPHESUS

To kick out the Persians from Anatolia just as he had kicked them out of Greece, Alexander with his strong army of 30.000 infantries and 5000 horsed men crossed the Dardanelles and reached Anatolia. From there he went to the city of Elaious, which is near Troy and there made an immolation by the tomb of Protesilaos who was the first man to set his foot ashore and to be killed. Then he made immolations by the tomb of Achilles and in the Athena Temple. When the Ionian Satrap, Spithridates, found out that Alexander was in Anatolia he set out with a strong army to stop him. According to Alexander's histograph Arrianos, army consisted of 40.000 infantries and 20.000 horsed men. The war which Arrianos called 'The War of the Horsemen' took place by the banks of the Granikos river and it did change the fate of antiquity. During the war, just as Spithridates was about to hit Alexander with his sword, he was killed by a Macedonian. Commander Mithridates, the son-in-law of Dareios was killed by a spear thrown by Alexander. Alexander who won this battle transferred the whole rights of the Satrap to Assandros, the son of Philatos. After a four days walk from Sardes, Alexander came to Ephesus. The greek hired soldiers who heard that the Persians were defeated and that the Satrap was killed, got hold of two persian galleys in the Ephesus harbor and fled. Alexander entered Ephesus without any resistance and said that he put an end to the governing of the persian minority and he announced that he established a new folk government. When the citizens of Ephesus started to attack the houses of the former governers and even started to kill them, Alexander stopped them from doing so. He then made a law which said that amount of tax paid to Persia should be given to the Artemis Temple instead. He offered immolations to Artemis and on his last day of stay he made a parade with his army.

On the night Alexander was born, a madman named Herostratos who wanted his name mentioned all throughout history, burned down the archaic Artemis Temple. Alexander visited the new Temple which was being built instead of the old one, he told that he wanted to pay all the expenses done for the Temple. But the citizens of Ephesus refused him politely by saying that it wouldn't be suitable for one God to give presents to another God.

After Alexander's death Ephesus was still, for sometime, under the reign of Assandros who was in Sardes. Eventhough in the year 313 B.C., Monoftalmos or Kyplop Antigonos took over the reign under the name of the Macedonian Kingdom, there was a big competition for the position all over Anatolia. The Empire fell into pieces. Antigonos (80) was defaeted and killed, by Lysimakhos in the Ipsos war and so Lysimakhos took over the reign of most of Anatolia (301 B.C.). According to Strabon, Lysimakhos rebuilt the Ephesus between the Pion and Koreses Mountains and the city walls which have remained in good shape until today and he named the çity Arsinoe, after his wife (287 B.C.). But the name could not gain any popularity among the citizens.

West Anatolia came under the riegn of Seleukos after the death of Lysimakhos (281 B.C.) in the Korupedian war. Ephesus accepted the reign of the Ptolemaiosans during the time of Anticochos Theos and then again accepted the Seleukosians in 196 B.C. In 188 B.C. Pergamum became the ruling king dom after the Apemeia peace.

Lysimachos Head

Attalos the third, became the king of Pergamon after the death of his uncle Attalos the 2nd. Eventhough Anatolia was in a of disorder during his reign Attolos did not fight any battles with anyone except for the Bithynians. It can be said that he did not interfere with the affairs of the State but he left this to other people he trusted. Because he was afraid of being killed he studied biology, zoology, pharmacology and especially the poisonous plants. In his testament he gave the kingdom over to Rome (133 B.C.) But his brother Aristonikos (who is of the same father but whose mother is a woman from Ephesus) did not accept this. First, the persuaded the slaves by promising them freedom and then he convinced the Royal Army in Phokaia. With the help of the Phokaian fleet he got hold of the coastal cities such as Colophon and Samos. While his fleet was awaiting him at the Kymle harbor it was attacked by the strong Ephesus fleet which was on the Roman's side, and it was destroyed. Even so the, revolt spread to the inner parts of Lydia. The army sent from Rome under the command of Lycinius Crassus Muciamis was defeated as well. Mucianus made one of the soldiers kill him. Another army sent in 130 under the command of Marcius Paperna was able to beat Aristonikos and so he added the lands of Anatolia to those of Rome.

After a short time in 129 B.C., because of the heavy taxes and the poor governing which arouse as a result of the Asia Province System, discontent began to show itsself in Asian countries. Because of this, Ephsus along with many other Anotilan cities, took place beside the Pontus King Mithridates the 6th who had rebelled against Rome. When Mithridates came to the Aegean Sea from the Blacksea with his strong fleet of 300 ships, every city welcomed him as the savivor. He ordered that every Roman or Roman originated person in Ephesus had to be killed (88 B.C.) Eighty thousand people were killed in one day. After this, Pergamon became the new capital of the

Ancient Settling Areas of Western Anatolia

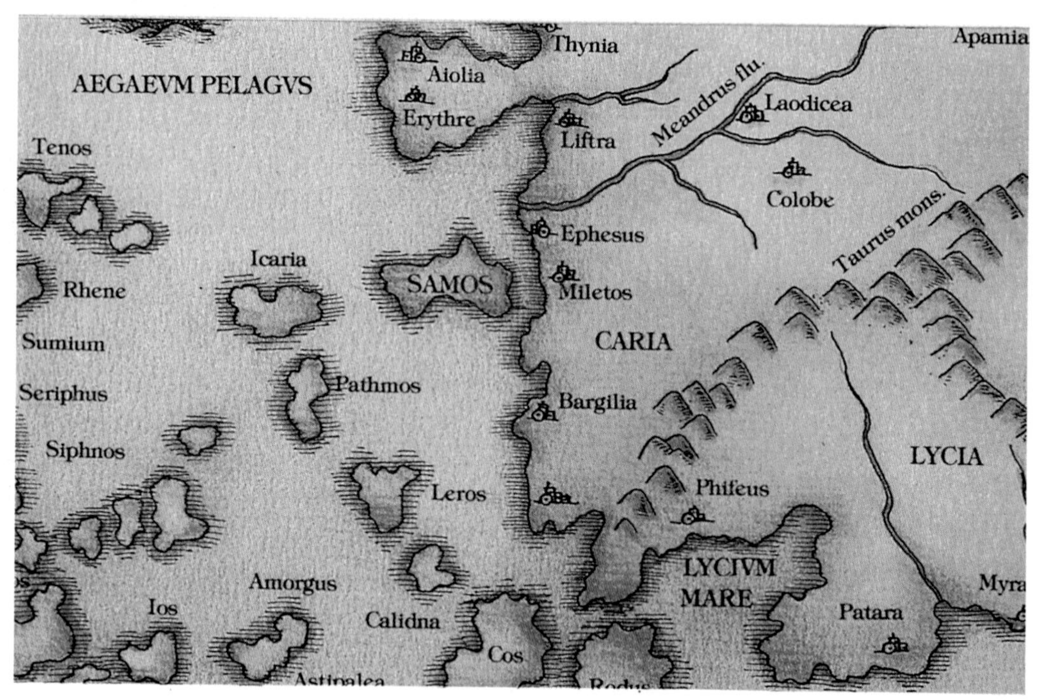

Pontus Kingdom. The Roman commander Aquillius who was taken prisoner, was famous for accepting bribe. He was sentenced to death by swallowing melted gold. In the same year the Pontusians took over Greece, too, but in 87 B.C. the Roman army under the command of Sulla took Athens back and marched to ward Roman army under the command of Sulla took Athens back and marched toward West Anatolia. Mithridates had to leave Pergamon because of the strong Roman Army and he was forced to move to Pitane which was another harbor. Meanwhile commander Lucillus, under the order of Sulla, with his fleet achieved many victories in Rhodes. Sulla whose intention it was to return to Rome and to supress the ones who were against him accepted the conditions of Mithridates and made an agreement with him. He took 3000 talens from him as war expenses. In addition he collected 20.000 talens from the other Anatolian cities to cover the expenses of the war he planned to fight in Rome. But the war did not come an end. Mithridates did not give in, although he was defeated many times. He continued the war after taking shelter by his son-in-law, a king in eastern Anatolia. Commander Lucullus fought Mithridates the 6th for many years who finally got one of the soldiers to kill him (63 B.C.) After this, the Roman armies that came to Asia, punished the ones who revolted against Commander Sulla and they bound the whole of West Anatolia to Rome.

A Commander Head A.D. 2nd. C.
Young Dionysos Statue (Detail) Roman Era

THE ROMAN EMPİRE ERA AND THE BYZANTIUM ERA

Antonius came to Ephesus after the Phillipoi war. The citizens of Ephesus who knew his fondness of the Dionysus festivals welcomed him in a festive way on the streets. Antonius sent his armies to Kilikia, when his relations with Octavianus were somewhat tense. He returned to Ephesus in 33 B.C. with Cleopatra. He there faught Octavianus in

Actium together with Cleopatra's fleet of 200 ships but he was defeated and so he returned to Egypt and beseiged Alexandria, first Antonius committed suicide out of despair and after him did Cleopatra. After this victory Octavianus became Emperor with the decision of the Senate and took the name Augustus (27 B.C.)

Augustus changed the capital from Pergamon again to Ephesus and turned it into the biggest, leading metropole. Thus Ephesus turned into a capital where the governor of Rome resided and at the same time it became an important trading center with a population of 200.000. It was one of the five biggest cities of the Roman Empire. Most of the remnants which are seen today are from the period of Augustus.

Emperor Hadrianus came to Ephesus twice. During his second visit in 129 A.D. he stayed for a while and supported the harbor-cleaning-project.

In 262 A.D. a Gothic fleet of 500 ships came from the east and crossed the Bosphorus and

Golden Woman Figurine

A General View of St. John Church.

they first plundered Kyzikos and then attacked Ephesus. They plundered and burnt the Artemis Temple which is considered as one of the seven wonders of the world.

The apostles whose duty it was to spread Christianity, were thrown out of Jerusalem after the year 37 A.D. One of the apostles, St. Paul, came to Ephesus in the year 53. For three years he tried to find supporters for the new religion. So Christianity started to spread in Ephesus. This situation bothered the people who were selling small Artemis statues. One of these, a jeweller called Demetrius, provoked the people and made them shout "The Artemis of Ephesus is supreme." for hours. The people continued the riot by taking Gaius, a friend of St. Paul's and others and took them to the theatre. St. Paul wanted to address the crowd but the people prevented him of doing so. Finally the guards told the people that the courts were open for those who wanted to complain. Thus the citizens calmed down and the crowd dispersed. After this St.Paul had to leave Ephesus and he headed towards Macedonia. Eventhough he later returned to Ionia he stayed in Miletos instead of Ephesus. In the year 64 his head was cut off outside the city walls of Rome. So, St.John became the head of the Ephesus church. During his crucifiction Jesus Christ pointed at St.John and said to Virgin Mary "Woman, this is your son." and then he turned to St. John and pointing out Mary he said "Man, this is your mother". and so he had trusted his mother to St. John. St. Paul's histograph Lucas does not mention Mary and St. John while explaing the events during the years 37-42 because at that time Mary and St. John were living in Ephesus. In the council reports of 431 A.D. it is said that Mary who came to Ephesus with St. John stayed at the Museion, which was the same place they stayed later, and that is the chapel of Virgin Mary.

Although he was very old, St. John travelled in Anatolia after he became head of the Ephesus church to spread Christianity against this religion was at its height in Pergamon and Smyrna, he was taken to Rome and exposed to torture. Later he was taken to Patmos where he wrote 'The Apocalypse'. The severe tortures in Rome to which the Christians were subject to, came to an end when Emperor Domitianus was stabbed to death by one of his servants. St. John came to Ephesus and wrote his Bible. According to his will he was buried in Ephesus and a chapel was built on him.

In 431 the council meeting was held in Ephesus. The main subject discussed during that meeting was the thesis that Mary was not the mother of God Christ but that she was the mother of Human Christ. The Constantinople Patriarch Nestorius came up with this idea during his stay in Antiocheia and when he returned to Constantinople he supported and tried to spread it more fiercly than before. Emperor Theodosius who became tired by the arguements aroused by the thesis asked for another meeting in the Virgin Mary church which was the first one built in her name. About 200 clergymen, among who were the Patriarch of Alexandria, Cyril, the Patriarch of Antiocheia, John and the representatitves of the Pope, attended the meeting. During the meeting which lasted three months, Ephesus went through some difficult days. It was during this meeting that the fact that Mary's grave was in Ephesus was put into official records.

When in the 4th century A.D. a basilica was built on St. John's grave, on the Ayasuluk Hill, some of the people of Ephesus settled around the Basilica. The beautiful days of the city which had become so crowded that it was almost impossible to use the harbor, had come to an end. Day by day Ephesus fell into more poverty. After Emperor justinian had built the St. John basilica, the Ayasuluk Hill became more and more important. After some time Ephesus became smaller and the population decreased. Because of this, new city walls were built and the defence area of Ephesus decreased as well.

During the 7th and 8th centuries A.D, the south and west Anatolia coasts were exposed to strong Arabic attacks. Meanwhile, because of the loss of unity in Anatolia, the city was filled with plunderers. Tha Ayasuluk castle was supported. Walls were built around the church. An important portion of the citizens settled within the walls.

The armies of the Calif Süleyman spent the winter of 716 in Ephesus.

When the Turks arrived there they found a very small community. The Seldjuk commander Caka Bey took the city without any resistance (1304). Later during the reign of the Aydınoğulları the name of the city was changed into Ayasuluk while it was Hagios Theololgos. When Ibn-i Batuta visited Ayasuluk in the 14th century he mentioned that it was a quite developed city and that there was the consulate of Cenova and of Venice and a bishop.

During the times of the Aydınoğulları reign, Ephesus again went through a prosperous period. The city was filled monumental mosques and baths and commerce became lively again. The famous Esabey Mosque is one of the pieces of that time (1374).

After the early Ottoman era, Ephesus was completely deserted.

Isabey Mosque

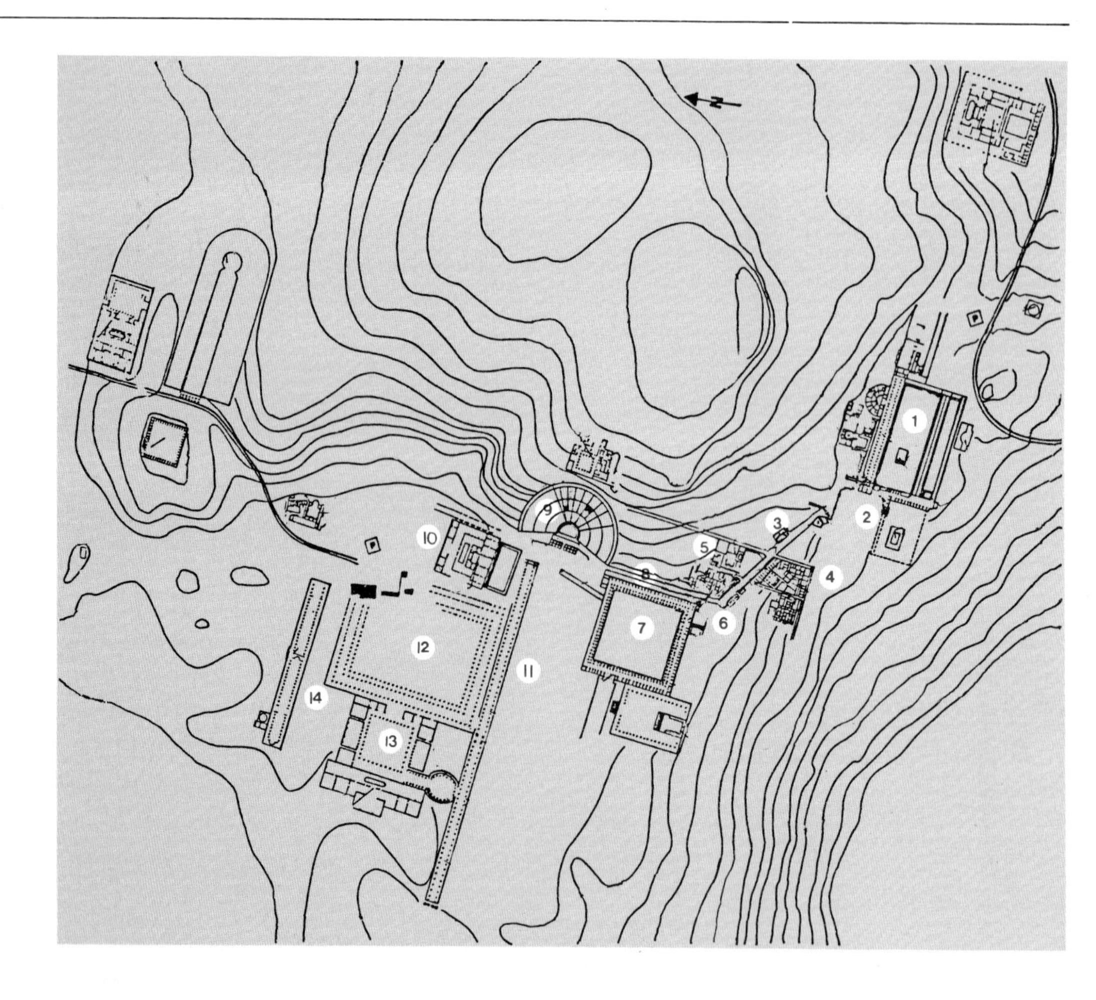

General plan of Ephesus
1) State Agora
2) Domitian place
3) Couretes street
4) Flank houses
5) Skolastika baths
6) Celsus Library
7) Commercial Agora
8) The Marble road
9) The Great Theatre
10) Theater Gymnasium
11) Harbor road
12) Harbor Gymnasium
13) Harbor baths
14) Council church

EXCAVATIONS

The city which has been forgotten with the flow of time again attains some importance when the Ayasuluk station along the Bagdat-Istanbul railway was built. The station was built to serve the Şirince village which lies 8 kms. to the east of Ephesus. Although the first excavations were made in 1869, there were still no more than a few houses around the station. In parallel with the progress of the excavations and tourism, the first Turkish Republican president Atatürk gave orders that the Turkish history should be researched thoroghly.

The first excavations was realized in 1869 by a British engineer called John T. Wood. He came to the region in 1863 and searched persistantly for the Artemis Temple which is mentioned quite often in ancient sources. He found it finally but he could not finish the excavation. The same excavation was continued by D.G. Hogart in 1904. The Artemis Temple and the altar in front of it are still being excavated by one of the Austrian Archeology Institute members, A.S. Bammer. The Institute started the excavations in 1895 after Otto Bendorf got permission from the Ottoman Emperor to do so. After Bendorf the excavation was conducted by Keil, Miltner, Eichler and Prof. Wetters. The Artemis Temple, the St. John church, the Council church, the Harbor Road, the Agoras, the Serapis Temple, the Celsus Library, the Theater, the Odeon, the Prythaneion Temple, the Marble Road and some of the houses have been dug out and some of them have been restored.

Since 1954 the management of the Ephesus Museum is also interested in environmental works as well as in excavations. Some of the environmental improvements of the Domitian Temple, the Theater, some of the Vedius Gymkasium the Stadium Road, the St. John church and the council Temple are still being conducted by the museum management.

Until the establishment of the Turkish Republic, the pieces found were transported to the British, Austrian and Istanbul Archeology Museums. With the Republic when it was prohibited to make these out of Turkey the findings were handed over to the Museum.

Excavation Workings, 1988

Remains of the City Walls

THE CITY-DEFENSE-WALLS

The walls built for the purpose of defense of Ephesus, surround the whole city. The ones best protected until today are the ones on the Pion mountain. The walls seen on the road of Mary's house and which belong to the Hellenistic era (3rd cent. B.C.) according to Strabon have been built by Lysimakhos while he was restoring the city. The walls built of even stone blocks are of 2m width and 6m height and are frequently supported with small, square shaped towers. The tower seen on the small hill towards the harbor is different from the others. It is bigger and it has two floors. Among the people this tower is called the St. Paul prison. The walls which come from way over the Pion mountain, make a turn here and continue towards the harbor.

There are two big gates in the walls from where the city can be entered and left. One of these is the Korressos Gate which is mentioned in inscriptions and which lies between the Stadium and the Vedius Gymnasium.
The second one is the Magnesia Gate which is on the road to Virgin Mary.

During the Byzantium era when Ephesus fell into poverty and the population decreased, the walls made smaller because the city was getting smaller and because it was difficult to defend the city with the walls of the Hellenistic period. The carelessly built walls seen in front of the Celsus Library and on the left of Harbor Road belong to that period. During the 1st and 3rd centuries during the Roman Peace era, the city did not have much importrance and so they were not looked after and subsequently some of them collapsed with earthquakes, and finally the lead and iron pieces that held the blocks together were taken which of course made the walls fall down.

THE MAGNESIA GATE

Magnesia was an important ancient city, 30 kms. to the east of Ephesus. The gate being placed at the beginnig of the road that lead from Ephesus to Magnesia thus got its name. The gate where excavations are still going on, was built in the 3rd century B.C. together with the Hellenistic walls. During the Roman Peace period the walls did not mean much so the name of the gate was changed into 'The Gate of Honor' by Emperor Vespasianus (69-79 A.D.) He made three entrances to the gate and gave it an arched look.

On both sides of the Hellenistic period gate were two square shaped high towers and on the city side there was a courtyard. The city could be entered through the second gate which came after the courtyard. Because the weakest points of the city defense were the gates, the enemy usually attacked those. If the gate would be opened the soldiers of the city (astactic) the enemy soldiers would find themselves in the courtyard and there they would be attacked by the soldiers waiting behind the second wall. The big square in front of the gate and courtyard was made of big gray stone blocks. In the square there are tombs which probably belong to important people. Because the city necropolis started immediately behind the walls, it must have been natural to place tombs up to the gates. The big water canal on the east of the square was built long after Emperor Vespasianus'es reign.

One end of the road that goes through the Magnesia Gate reaches Magnesia, on the other side it winds up the mountain and reaches the Artemis Temple turns back to Ephesus (being its main street) and the ends again at the Magnesia Gate. According to an inscription the road has been restored by the sage Damianus of Ephesus in the 2nd century A.D. Because the city was built after the plans of Hippodamus, a Miletian architect, all streets are perpendicular. But the road mentioned above does not follow this rule. The reason of this that the road which has lead to the Temple for a long time and which has thus been considered sacred was not included in the new city plan made during

Defense Wall of the City

Olimpia Tomb Stele - From Magnesia Door Finds

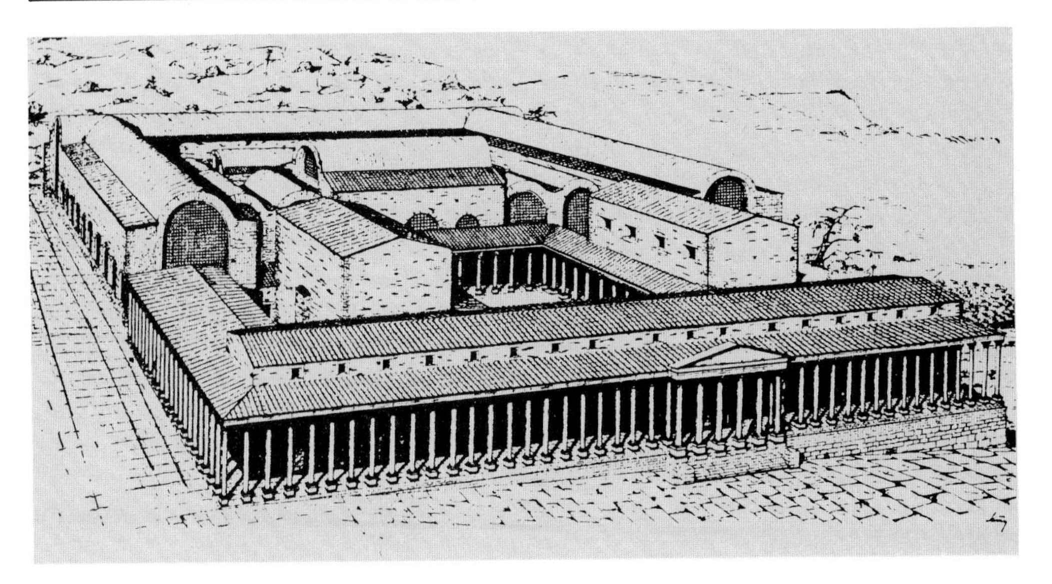

Reconstruction of the Eastern Gymnasium (up)

Lysimakhos'es period. Wood found the Artemis Temple by following this road. He got the information from an inscription.

THE EASTERN GYMNASİUM

The wide-spread ruins seen on the Pion mountain side of the Magnesia gate belong to the building called the EASTERN GYMNASTUM. Because many young-girl statues were found during the 1930-31 excavations, it is also called the Girl's Gymnasium. The building faced the holy road passing in front of it and it was made by the Sage Flavius Damianus in the 2nd century. A.D. These gymnasiums which were made for the purpose of education and sports were somewhat like the boarding schools of today. Boys between 6-16 could attend the school for education. Subjects taught were sports, music astronomy, medicine and fine speech. The very bright students could continue their education for many years.

The Eastern Gymnasium which is a monumental building was a complete one with its bath, paleistra, class rooms and the Emperor's Hall. The entrance on the east side is columned and has triangular pediments. In front there was a row of stores with columns in front of them. The statues of Damianus and Vedia Phaedrina which are exhibited at the İzmir Archeological museum were found in this gymnasium. Between the gymnasium and the asphalt road, a church was built during the Byzantium period. Only the base and the floor mosaics of this beautiful church have remained until today.

The round building seen on the left on the way walking from the gymnasium to the car-park is known as the St.Lucas church. The building which is 1m. above the ground and which a diameter of 16 ms. is surrounded with marble plates. The crucifixes on the plates have been engraved later and thus have lead to the wrong conclusion that this was the St. Lucas church. But according to archeological finidings the building was built 100 years before St. Lucas, the histogrph of St. Paul.

General View of Ephesus (on the reverse page)

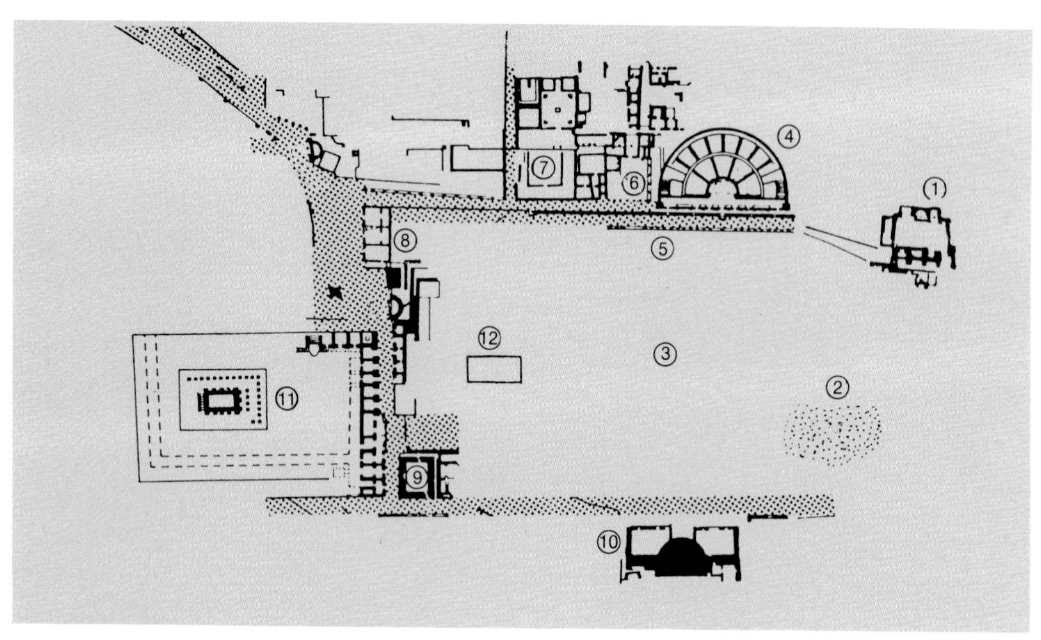

The Architectural Plan of the Sate Agora

1) The Varius Bath
2) Necropol
3) Square of the Agora
4) Odeon
5) Basilica
6) Dea Roma Temple
7) Prytaneion
8) Fountaion of Pollio
9) Gaius Laecanius-Bassus Fountain
10) South Hall
11) Domitian Temple
12) Issis Temple (Augustus Temple)

THE STATE AGORA

The wide smooth open space seen on the right hand-side on the way from the Museum entrance is the Ephesus State Agora. Not many remnants are left. The measures of the Agora are 160x56 m. On the Pion Mountain side of the Agora there is a marble road, on the Panayır mountain side is a Basilica, the Vaious bath, the Odeion and the Prythaneion. The State Agora was a half-sacred place where political, social and religicus meetings were held, under the control of the state. Like in many other Agoras, there wes a square shaped temple in the middle of this one, too. The Temple was ruined very much and its construction elements were used for the restoration of other buildings.

When places having to do with water were found around it, it was firstly suggested that this might have been the Isis Temple but then it was supposed to be the Augustus Temple. The group of statues explairing Odyssei's adventures with Polyphemos which were found on the pediment of the Temple, were later put beside the round planned Pollio fountain. The Temple was made together with the Agora in the 1st century. B.C. Drillings made at the Agora showed that there were remnants of a former one, 1,5-2 m below the present one. During a 3m. drill, remnants of the road surrounding the Panayır mountain (dated back to the 6th cent. B.C.) and tombs made of soil and tombs made of soil and which are called the Closomenai type were found. One of the tombs is exhibited at the Tomb Remnants Hall of the Ephesus Museum.

The State Agora took its last shape during Emperor Theodusius'es period (379-395 A.D.) On its north and east were two stoas which have remained until today.

Remains of State Agora (up) and Columns of Agora (down)

THE BASILICA

The stoa on the north of the Agora was changed into a basilica in Augustus'es period. The Basilica which is 160m. long had a wooden roof. Today only some of the columns are left.

During the Augustan period the captions of the columns were in Ionic style having bull-heads but during the late Empire period they were changed into Corynthian style. It was found out later during the excavation that the stoa on which the Basilica was built had a depth of 1.30m.

Through another smaller stoa on the east it was possible to enter it from three different doors. The stoa underwent some changes during the Bizantyne period and lost its importance. The statues of Augustus and his wife Livia which are exhibited in the Emperor's Hall of the Museum were found there The statues were ruined and there was a crucifix on both of the foreheads.

A General View from the Basilica-Columns of the Basilica

Remains of Varius Bath

THE VARIUS BATH

It is the first building on the north of the Basilica. The walls up to the vaults have remained in very good shape. Although the excavations have been continuing since 1929 they have not been finished yet. In order to build the bath, the Panayır mountain has been smoothened and the shaved rocks onthe mountain side have been used as walls. It has the classical design of all Roman baths. Main sections such as the frigidarium (cold section) the tepidarium (warm section) and the caldarium (hot saction) are side by side The sections on the sides, cover a wide space. The walls are made of big limestone blocks. The vaulted roof is made of bricks. The conduit pipes which are in the wall of the tepidarium and caldarium make it possible for the hot air to travel around. The remnants of the hypocaust of the caldarium have remained in very good shape until today.

The bath has been enlarged with additional buildings, and has been changed during the Roman, and Bizantyne periods. The mosaic covered room is an example to this and it was added in the 5th century. A.D. According to an inscription found in the building, P.Flavius and his wife had a private hall made there for themselves.

THE ODEİON

It is next to the Varius Bath an looks like a small theater. So, it is also called the small theater. It was built as a Bouleterion by Publius Vedius Antonius and his wife Flavia Papania; people from a very elite family. It was used as an odeon. The political system consisted of two parlaments. One was the 'Demos' (public) parlament which consisted of the whole Ephesus population and which held its meetings in this BigTheater, the other one was the Consulting Parlament (also called the Boule) which consisted of 300 members and which held its meeting at the Odeion.

There are 23 rows in the Cavae of the Odeion. It is divided into two equal parts with a diezome. It could take 1400 people. The audience would go down to the diazome through a staired and from there they would reach their seats. The excavations and restorations of the east part of the gallery have been completed. The orchestra was in front of the cavea in a semi-circle. The absence of a water outlet can be evidenca that Odeion was a covered building. The stage is two-floored. Right in front of it, there is marble podium. There were five doors to the podium. The one in the middle is wider and higher than the others. The building took the name Odeion because it was more often used as the odeion for concerts.

THE TEMPLES OF DEA ROMA AND JULİUS CAESAR

Emperor Augustus gave permission to the non-Roman citizens of the state to make an Augustus Cult. The cult for the Bithynia State was in Nicomedia and for the Asia State in Pergamon. Other than these two cults for the adoptive father Augustus, Divius Julius Caesar who was announced god by the Senate and for Dea roma were built in Nicaea and Ephesus for the Roman citizens. These two temples were built right next to the Odeion (4-14 A.D.) On their east sides they have four columns each. In later periods different buildings for different purposes were built on the same spots and so the Temples were completely destroyed. Today we can only see the marble podium and the walls which are only as high as the foundation.

Columns of Dea Roma Temple

Eros Head. Roman Era Copy from the Lysippos' Original

PRYTHANEION

The most religious and responsible managerial duty which could be obtained in Ephesus was Prythanism. The most important duty of the Prythan who would be of an élit family, would be to look after the immortal fire, the hearth of the city, so that it would never go out neither day nor night. The Prythan would do this very proudly in the name of the hearth Goddess Hestia. Other important duties of the Prythan would be to look after the different cults of the city and to take care of the daily sacrifices. The expenses needed for these were covered by the Prythan. The Artemis Temple was left out of the city, in other words out of the Prythan's management system. The Temple had within itsself its own system.

The Ephesus Prythaneion is on the west side of the Basilica. Other than the buildings on its side, it had a courtyard in the front and a big hall at the back. It resembled a Temple because there were eight, thick and tall columns in the front, of which two can still be seen today. The inside of the Prythaneion was also built in a pompous way. At the corners of the building there were columns and two of those had sections in the shape of hearts. The hearth which burned day and night was there and it was called 'The Holy Place of Hestia. The altar was at the very middle of this place but today only the base made of basalt is left.

The inscriptions an the columns and the architectural pieces give the list of the 'Currettes Union'. The Currettes were a class of monks who belonged to the Artemis Temple. First there used to six currettes but then the number was increased to nine The Currettes Union belonged to the Temple only until the Hellenistic period but with Emperor Augustus the Currettes obtained a place in the Prythaneion. The main duty of the Union was to celebrate the birth of Artemis in a dramatic way at Ortygia which is on the south-west of Ephesus. Eventhough the Prythaneion was first built in the 3rd century B.C., it took its final shape during the reign of Augustus. When the building collapsed, probobly in an earthquake inthe 4th century, the construction elements were taken to the Scholastica and used for its restoration.

Prytaneion and its columns with Inscription

Flying Nike Relief with wreath

THE DOMITIAN SQUARE

There is a road that leads from the Prythaneion to the Domitian Square and on both sides of the road there are pedestals with figures on them. The one on the left shows God Hermes who with one hand is holding the horns of a ram and with the other a caduceus which is his symbol. On the other sides of the pedestal there is a tripot and underneath it, is a snake. On the pedestal on the right we can again see Hermes who is holding a ram by its horn. On the other side there is a tripot under which there is a piale. The purpose of neither of the pedestals is known.

Some parts of the Domitian Square have been dug. The architectural marble columns seen in the middle of the square belong to the surrounding buildings. The circular memorial, ornamented with girlands and which is in the very middle of the columns was brought here in the 4th cent. A.D. from another part of the city and was put there negligently. Right beside this there is a flying Nike, holding a wreath, in high-relief. This triangular architectural piece belongs to the Heracles Gate at the beginning of the Currettes Road. From the Square there is southward, narrow road that leads to the Pion Mountain. On the Agora side of the road there are two-floored vaulted, various stores and buildings which were used for various purposes. The west side of the stores has not been excavated yet.

Base with Hermes Figure (right)

Monument of Memmius - Blocks with caius and Sulla Reliefs.

THE MEMMIUS MEMORIAL

It is on the north side of the square and it looks like a four sided victory arch. The pedestal is made of domestic round stones, the top is made of marble. The memorial is on a three-staired krepis which comes after the pedestal. On each side there are semi-circular pedestals which are tied together with belts and above the niches there are figured blocks. Most of these blocks are lost. The soldier figures seen are Memmius, his father Caius, and his grandfather dictator Sulla.

The latin inscription seen on the east side of the building reads as follows: "Caius Memmius, the son of Caius, the grandson of Cornelius Sulla, the Savior." This memorial was built in the 1st century A.D.

Pollio Fountain (up)
Head of Zeus, A finding of Pollio fountain (down)

THE POLLIO FOUNTAIN

It is on the side of the square that faces the Agora. It is a very pompous building with its very wide and high arch. The arch used to carry a triangular pediment. The water used to come from the semi-circular exedra by the Agora. The polyphemus statues group which is now being exhibited at the Ephesus museum, was on the top of this round wall of the pool. These statues which formerly used to be the pediments of the Augustus (Isis) Temple in the center of the Agora, were placed here probably because of some destruction. The statues tell about the adventures of Polyphemos, a son of Poseidon, after the Troian wars.

According to inscriptions the fountain was built in 97 A.D. by Sextillius Pollio.

From Pollios Fountain Finds, Polypheuos Statue Group belonging to the Pediment of Augustus Temple.
Resting Warrior (down)

Torso of Aphrodit

Dominitian Temple

THE DOMITIAN TEMPLE AND THE EMPEROR'S CULT

Ephesus, during the antiquity, obtained four times the right to build the Neaocoros, in other words the Emperor's Temple. To have an Emperor's Temple in the city was a distinguished honor. This right was given to Ephesus by Emperor Domitianus for the first time (81-96 A.D.). To show their gratitude, they put a 5m. high statue of the Emperor in front of the Temple which they had built on a 50x100m terrace which was placed at the south corner of the square. Some pieces of the statue, which together with its pedestal is 7m. high, are in the Ephesus Museum. The head which is in good shape is in the Izmir Archeological Museum.

Eventhough there is not much left of the Temple, it is possible, by looking at the ruins, to guess how it was planned.. According to those it was set on a podium to which there were eight stairs. The measures of the podium were 24x34m. On each of the long sides there were 13 and at the front and back sides there were 8 columns on each side. There were four columns on its pronaos. The altar being 10 meters in front of the Temple was a cornered "U" and it was staired. Some parts of it are exhibited in the Emperor's Hall of the Ephesus Museum.

After Emperor Domitianus was slain by one of his servants, the loss of the hard obtained Neocoros came into question. As a solution the citizens of Ephesus announced the father of the Emperor, Vespasianus, a God and vowed the Temple to him. So Ephesus saved its prestige against its most important enemies, Pergamon and Smyrna.

The second time the right was given by Emperor Hadrianus. When Hadrianus came from Athens to Ephesus as Zeus Olympos, the citizens built the Temple, in Olypeion, of which only the base under the earth is left. This Temple which is close to Mary's church is the fourth biggest Temple in Turkey.

During the years 211-212 when Emperor Caracalla was ruling the country with his brother Geta, Ephesus got the third permission to build an Emperor's Temple. When Caracalla killed his brother in 212 he addressed the citizens and said that he gave up the Temple in favor of Artemis.

From the decisions of the Roman Senate we learn that Ephesus obtained the fourth permission during the period of Emperor Valerianus (251-260 A.D.)

For the cities of the antiquity, to have an Emperor's Temple was a great honor. Ephesus did everything not to loose the lead to Pergamon or Smyrna. These Emperor Temples were under the care and management of the priests called Arkhierus. All the arkhieruses were responsible to the Asiarchs. Being an archierus required a lot of financial sacrifices but it was a very honoring duty. It was closely related with gladiator games, wild animal fights, the Emperor Cult and the celebrations of the cult. The rich families of Ephesus, like the Vediuses, founded special gladiator schools for such games.

The Emperor's Cult was never a religion in the real sense. This cult was more of an institution to protect and bring together the people of Rome without discriminating, culture, and religion.

Marble Altar - From the Finds of Dominitian Temple.

Gallery of Written Documents

WRITTEN DOCUMENTS

On the side of the Domitian Temple which faces the square there is a row of well preserved stores. In the center of these there are stairs which lead to a beautiful terrace. In front of the same side there is a parabet made of two-floored columns. This parabet makes up the border of this side and it also adds a different touch. The terrace, has an arched underground structure, as do many buildings which are set on sloped grounds. This 154m. long "U" shaped underground structure is called 'Kripto Portik". The ends of the Kripto Portik which surround the bottom of the Temple, open up to the Domitian Square from above the stores. The east side was rearranged as the gallery of written documents and thus the opportunity of exhibiting the more important ones of the 2000 inscriptions found during the excavations, aroused.

The inscription numbered four is about death penalties given to religious crimes. It tells about the 44-46 people who treated the intermediaries sent from Ephesus and who were bringing gifts to the Artemis Temple of Sardes, badly, and that these people plundered the gifts as well.

The inscription number 11, dated 3-4 century B.C., reads as follows: "This wall, up to the roof, is the common property of Moshkion and Eucleides" Thus, collective ownership is being mentioned.

In the inscription number 13, King Attalos praises the citizens of Ephesus by the name of an Ephesusian educater working in the Pergamon castle. This educater whose name was Aristo, was educating Attalos 111., the king-to-be of Pergamon.

The inscription number 27, lists the rules to be followed during the immolation ceremonies held by the Prythan.

In number, 31, Emperor Hadrianus is named Zeus Olympios. This inscription was erected during Hadrianus'es arrival from Athens to Ephesus.

Columns of Dominitian Temple with Cariatid

DC1

Statues of Nymphes 2nd. C. A.D.

THE GAIUS LAECANIUS BASSUS FOUNTAIN

It is on the southwest corner of the State Agora. The building which was made facing the Domitian Temple and the street infront of it, is two-floored and columned. The columns put on each floor are in doubles. Among these are niches and on the niches there are statues having to do with water, such as tritons and nyphes and these are still being exhibited at the Ephesus Museum. In front there is a small pool. Its measures are 13x8m. The two sides of the pool are two-floored and columned. According to the inscription this fountain was built by Gaius Laeciauns Bassus in 75-80

THE HERACLES GATE

It is on the beginning of the Currettes Road which leads from the Domitian Square to the Celsus Library. It has two floors. Its bottom floor is arched. The top floor has six columns in a row. On the pedestals which were at the corners there are nikes in high-relief. These are exhibited in the Domitian Square. One of these, and most of the construction elements of the building could not be found. On the two middle columns, of the six mentioned above, there are two Heracles Statues in high-relief. He is presented wrappad up in the hide of the Nemea Lion. These columns have been put under the today non-existing arch of the gate, in order to give information. These materials show a 2 century A.D. style. They must have been taken from another part of the city in the 4 century and put there.

Heracles Door - Victory Arch (right)

TG2

A General wiew from the Currettes road

THE CURRETTES ROAD

The currettes who were considered half-gods have always been treated with ultimate respect by the citizens of Ephesus because the currettes had been very helpful during the birth of Artemis. This class of priest which has been established to celebrate the birth at Ortygia (the place where Artemis was born) was called the 'Union of Currettes'. Later the currettes obtained their place in the Prythaneion and their names were engraved on its columns and on other architectural materials. The road which leads from the Heracles Gate to the Celsus Library has been named the Currettes Road. Many monumental buildings, were fecing this road because it was at the center of the city. The floor is covered with marble plates and the columned galleries on the sides are covered with ornamental mosaic. Some of these have been restored. The marble plates and columns were first used for other purposes and brought here later. Some of the columns are thinner some are winder and some are of different color. The road had been destroyed with the earthquake in 17 A.D. but restored with much care. But then because of the frequent earthquakes in 355, 365 and 368 A.D. it was ruined completely like many other buildings. Later it was restored very carelessly with materials of other buildings not used anymore. The door of the stores, houses and other building opened up to the gallery. On the pedestals which can be seen between the columns there were statues of the people who had done very helpful things for the city. The inscripted statue which is next to the Heracles Gate is one of those and belongs to the physician Alexandros. The deeds and personality of Alexandros are unknown. The statue of Council Stephanos, which is also exhibited in the Emperor's Hall of the Ephesus Museum, was also found here.

THE TRAIAN FOUNTAIN

Young Dionysos - Traian Fountain Find (up)

It is on the north side of the Currettes Road. According to its inscription it was built during 102-114 A.D. and dedicated to Emperor Traian (98-117 A.D.).This immolation inscription is on the big cornie beside the fountain. On the inscription the word Ephesus is preceeded by the word Neocoros which was used as a means of showing pride. The fountain which has been restored but reduced in size, has a front made of two-floored columns. The statues of Dionysus, satyrs and Aphrodite found on the niches among the columns are being exhibited at the Hall of Fountain Findings, the Ephesus Museum. On the center niche which is a bit wider than the others, is the Statue of the Emperor. The pedestal of the Statue and some pieces of the foot are in their original place. The water to the pool came from the canal under the statue of the Emperor.

Remains of Traian Fountain

Entrance of Scolastica Bath and Christian Scolastica Statue (up)
Caldarium of Scolastica Bath. (down)

THE SCHOLASTICA BATH

The baths, during the Roman period, were places that had their own rules and were visited by everybody, rich or poor. Some baths would not charge the poor so that they could use the bath as well. The rich would prefer to go there with their slaves and would stay there for a long time. One would first undress at the apoditerium and then perspire at the sudotorium and at the section called the caldarium servants would bathe and massage their masters. After the bathing daily matters, philosophy and politics were discussed at the tepidarium. And finally came the swimming, in the cool pool of the frigidarium, in order to relax. After the Romans, baths lost their importance and in the middle-ages they were completely forgotten. But they again became important during the Seldjuk and Ottoman periods.

The Scholastica bath which is placed next to the Traian Fountain is the largest building among the ones alike. Together with the ground floor it has three floors but the third floor is totally ruined. It has two entrances. One is on the Currettes Road the other one is on the road perpendicular to the Currettes Road. The first hall is the apoditerium. The wall of the hall, which is adjacent to the road is columned. The apoditaruium is columned and niched. The statue seen on one of the columns, belongs to Christian Scholastia who had the bath restored for the last time towards the end of the 4th century. A.D. The frigidarium is the hall on the west of the apoditarium and it has an ecliptical pool in the center. The door on the north leads to the tepidarium. In the walls and floor of this section (there are ceramic pipes) which contain hot air to heat the place. The marbla mosaic seen a few centimeters below the surface on the east wall of the tepidarium belong to the original coating of the Bath. When the bath was restored by Christian Scholastica the ground was covered anew with marble plates. The tepidarium leads to the caldarium through a small and narrow door. This section has been preserved up to its original height. The round legs seen under the ground cover were there to hold up this ground and so the hot air would be sent to various places through those legs. The hot air would come from the hippocaust on the west wall.

THE LATRINA

It is on the narrow and vaulted street which is on the west of the Scholastica Bath. This building, which was a public toilet had a pool without a roof and it had a square shape. The toilets were placed side by side on the wall. The floor of the Latrina is covered with colored mosaic. It was first built in the 1st century. A.D. but was restored many times until the 4th century.

Latrine

Relief Bust of Tyche

THE HADRIANUS TEMPLE

It is one of the most beautiful buildings on the Currettes Road. It is estimated that it was built in 138 A.D. The architecture of the front wall and pronao isvery elaborate but the nao is very plain. The nao is made up of small stones. In front of the pronao there are 4 columns with corynthian captions that carry the triangular frontals. These frontals form an arch, like Syrian frontals, on the two middle columns. On the center stone of the arch the statue of the goddess of the City, Tyche, is seen.

With respect to the smallness of the Temple the doors are very huge and their beams are decorated richly with classical designs such as rows of pearls and eggs. On the semi-circular second frontal is a nude Medusa figure among leaves and flowers.

The original friezes on the both sides of the upper beam found on the door of the pronoa is in the Ephesus Museum. Copies were placed here during restoration. The subjects of the first three friezes (from the left) are: Some Gods and Goddesses, the chasing of a bore by the horsed ktistes of Ephesus, Gods and Amazons, Amazons and the Dionysus procession. The subject of the fourth frieze is different than the others. There is Athena, Selena, an unknown man, Apollo, a woman, Androcles, Heracles, the father of Theodosius, Emperor Theodosius, the Artemis of Ephesus, the wife and son of Theodosius and the Goddess Athena. The Temple which has been ruined by the earthquake in the middle of the 4th century. A.D. has been restored. During the restoration the fourth frieze has been redone and put there. The Temple has been dedicated to Emperor Hadrianus by P.Quintillus in 138 A.D. The four incripted pedestals seen in front of the Temple's columns belong to the four emperors who owned the Imperium Romanum at the same dates. As seen on the inscription these are: Diocletian, Maximian, Constantinus Chlorus and Gallerius (293-305 A.D.)

Front wiew of the Hadrianus Temple (left)

Medusa Figure

A Detail from Pronaos Friezes - Gods and Amazons (down)

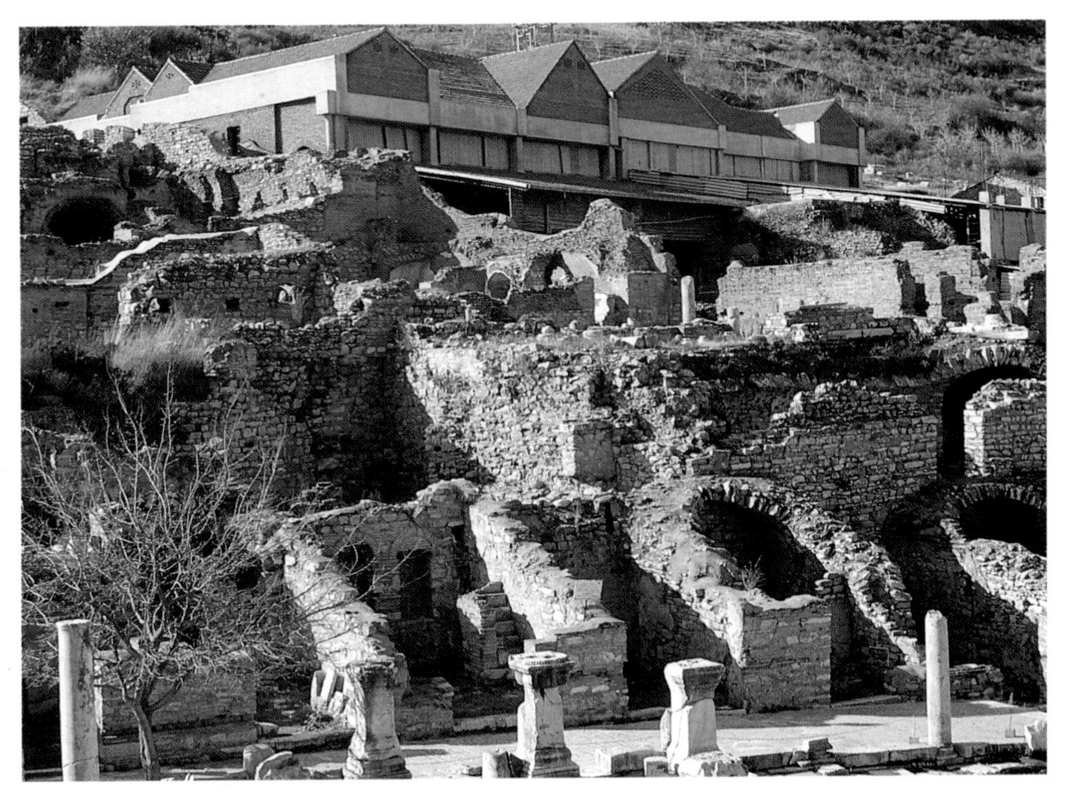

Front wiew and the entrance steps of the flank houses from Currettes road.

THE FLANK HOUSES

The houses which are placed on the flank across the Hadrianus Temple are called "The Flank Houses" or they were called "The Houses of the Rich" because they were in the center of the city and inhabited by the rich and élite people. The narrow, and in some parts staired, steep streets which are perpendiculer to the Currettes Road were the connection of the houses to the Road. On each terrace along the streets was a door of each house. All houses were perystilled (with small courtyards). The rooms and halls were placed around it. The light would be obtained by the peristyle which would be uncovered. And because naturally this light wouldn't be enough, the inner rooms would be dark ahd dim.

There would be a well and reservoir in each house. But the whole city had its running water. Each house had its taps; some had eve two, and one would definitely be in the peristyle. The water would come to the city cistern by ducts and from there it would be lead to the marble distribution tank which was as big as a small tomb. And so it would be possible to distribute enough water to each house. The various holes of different diameters made it possible for the landlords to take as much water a they wanted. These wholes can be resembled to the water counters of today.

The ceramic pipes seen on the walls and floors of some houses had to do with heating. The bath of the house which had the same system of the city bath thus, would provide hot air to any place needed. The bathroom could be used by several people at once because of the numbers of toilets in it. Each toilet had its washbasien in front of it.

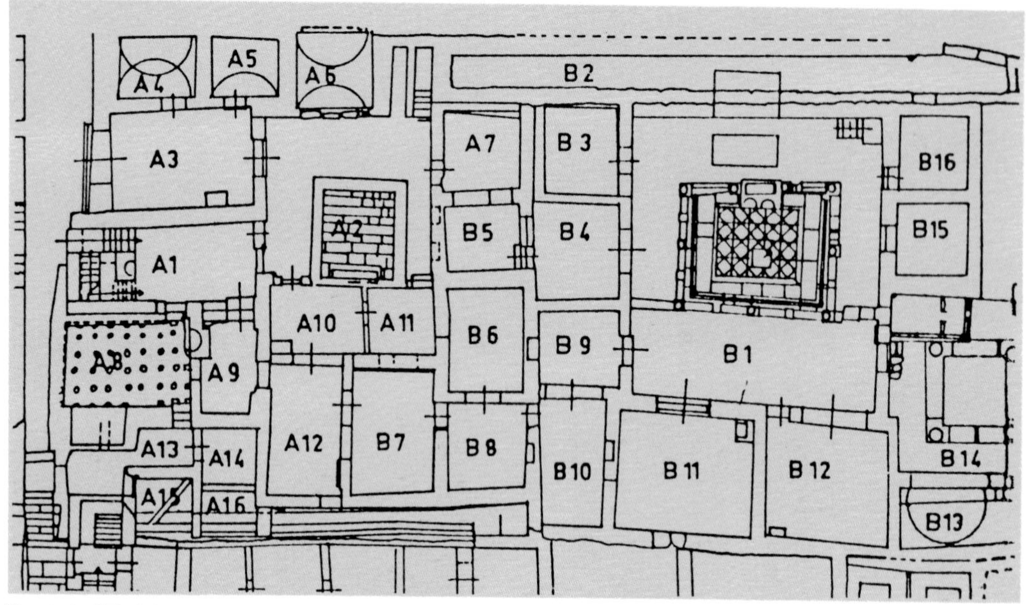

The plan of Flank houses, peristyle A and B

Eventhough the houses had several floors, only the first floors of the houses remained until today and the upper floors were completely destroyed. The bedrooms were on the top floors, the ground floors were for living, dining and guests. The kitchen, toilet, bath, and servant rooms were on the bottom floor.

The floors of the rooms were decorated with geometrical and mythical mosaic designs. The walls would be ornamented with-colored flower, fish, bird designs, Cupid, Muse, mythical masks, figures representing scenes of plays, so that there would be no empty spot on the walls. The most important characteristics of the Flank Houses were the frescos. Their base colors would usually be dark red but the designs and figures would be of various colors. Within time they have been redone over and over again. In some houses it was possible to count seven layers of frescos. It is quite clear that the frescos would be made according to the fashion of the day. In some places the frescos are covered with colored marbles. But because cutting the marbles very thinly was extremely difficult and very expensive people would prefer marble-imitation-frescos.

The excavations show that these houses were built during the period of Augustus but they were constantly restored and changed until the end of the 6th century. But because they were not used anymore after the 7th century they were filled with soil and rubble. Later water mills were built on top of these houses on the west end and these were used for a long time.

THE 1. PERISTYLED HOUSE

The original entrance of the house is from the staired street across the Hadrianus Temple. From the two doors which open up to this street, the one below was used for service and the upper and smaller one was used for everyday entrances. The house has been restored in such a way that it can give an overall idea of all of the Flank Houses. It has two floors. One of the stairs is right beside the everyday door, the other one is on the southwest corner of the peristyle. The second floor is completely ruined. The house which built on 900m², had twelve rooms for various usages. After the door were a few stairs which lead to the entrance hall (A 1). The fountain with the groove was put there after the original construction. The hall leads to the peristyle through an arched wide door (A 2). The peristyle has four columns and the ground is covered with marble. Between the two columns on the south there is a very much ruined fountain. The A 10-11 sections behind the fountain have floors covered with mosaics and walls with frescos. Eventhough the house itsself was built in the 1st century. A.D. these two rooms were added later during the changes in the 4th century. To the east of the peirstyle there is a well preserved hall (A 3) whose walls are 4m. high. On both sides of its door there are frescos which have to do with drama scenes, and so this room is also called the 'Theater Room'. Because the actors of the Roman period used masks the actors here were also presented with masks. On the right is a scene from the comedywriter menander's play 'Sicyonoi' and on the left there are scenes from Euripides'es 'Orestes' and 'Iphigenia'. The north and south walls of the theater room are ornamented with normal sized, nude men and women figures. It is difficult to tell who they are. On the top of the north wall there is a Heracles-Akheleos fight. Akheleos who is the most important God of the rivers of West Greece, wants to marry Deineira, the daughter of the Caledon King. Deineira gets scared of Akheleos because he can change into a bull, dragon or anyother creature he wants, and she wantsto marry Heracles. So Akheleos turns himself into a dragon and fights Heracles. This is the story of the fresco. The floor of the theater room is completely covered with mosaics. The walls of the two adjacent rooms which open up to the Theater Room are covered with floral frescos. The mosaics and frescos of the Theater Room are dated 2nd century A.D.

The bath is on the south of the entrance hall (A 8). The floor marbles are totally destroyed but the round high legs which carried the marbles and among which the hot air used to travel, still remain. The ruins of the basin niches right by the entrance of the bath remain, too. Not much of the kitchen is left, it is actually completely ruined. The small buildings around are food storages and the door that opens up to the outside is the service door. After the kitchen there is a row of rooms whose floors the last one of these rooms leads to the second peristyled house.

Orestes Fresco (up)

Fresco of the Fight of Heracles to Acheloos (up) and
Detail from the Base Mosaic of the Peristyle of House A

The peristyle of House A and House B

THE 2ND PERISTYLED HOUSE

The house with two peristyles is larger than the former. In the first peristyle there are six thin columns with corynthian captions. Right in the middle is the cistern with its original cover and the south side is its fountain which must have had two faucets. The columns on the south belong to the later restorations of the house, and were found the way they are today.

The niche (B 6) which faced the southwall of the peristyle for the landlord to rest. The floor marbles are black and white and designed in a straw beading fashion. The vault is decorated with glass mosaic in which blue is the dominant color. The center figures of the mosaic are: Ariadne and Dionysus, around them are white birds. The mosaic was made during a restoration in the 5th century A.D.

In front of the vaulted niche is a footplate and there is a colored mosaic Triton who in his left hand holds a fork, the symbol of his father Poseidon and in his right hand he holds the halter of a hippocampus on which a Nereid is sitting. On the west side of this hall are stairs which lead to the second floor. On each side of this hall there are two rooms which open up to the big hall with the mosaic floor. The ones on the east (B 9-10) have panels on their walls which are ornamented with muses and on which names are written. These sections which were somewhat larger than the ones in the north, were used as dining rooms (D 11-12).

The floor mosaics in all other parts of the house have been replaced with larger pieces of mosaics during the restoration The Kitchen is on the west side and is fairly small. It has fish frescos on its wall. The door beside the kitchen opens up to the second peristyle (B 14) Right next to the basin which is on the west corner, there is the bathroom of the house which is again for a number of people. This house was built in the 1st century A.D. but went through many changes. Most of the frescos seen on the walls were made during the restorations in the 4th century A.D.

Amphirite and Triton. Mosaic

Dionysos and Ariadne. Mosaic (up)
Fresco of a bird (down)

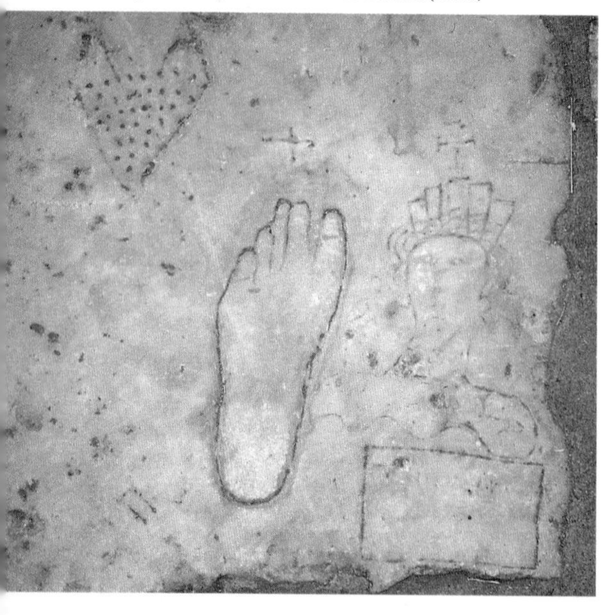

Little Statue of Priaphos (up)
Sign Showing the Direction of Brothel (down)

THE LOVE HOUSE

The building behind the Hadrianus Temple and the Bizantyne Stoas is known as the Love House of Ephesus. The house resembling the Flank Houses and two floors and a peristyle. It is estimated that it was planned in 98-117 by Emperor Traian together with the public toilets and the Scholatica Bath and that is was restored together with the other buildings in the 4th century and that it was used until the 7th century. The second floor is completely destroyed. Eventhough the walls on the ground floor. were all covered with frescos only very few of them remain. The room on the west and whose floor has the four seasons mosaic figures, is the dining room. Right next to it is the small bath of the house. Again on the west side there is an eclitical pool with a mosaic ground. This mosaic shows three women who are taking drinks, a maid, a rat that is eating the left-over bread and a cat. On the Currettes Road side of the house there is a well whose water is still used today. In the Fountain Findings Hall of the Ephesus Museum there is a Priapos staute with a big phallos, which has been found in the well.

THE OCTAGON

Right across the Hadrianus Temple there is a tomb memorial of which only the pedestal and the underground tomb-room are left. The memorial was made in 40-20 B.C. Because the statues and inscriptions of the people who did favorable things for Ephesus were put along the main streets it was also customary to build tomb memorials of important people in the city center. The Octagon is one of them. It has an eight cornered shape and a pyramid-like roof. Around it is a row of corynthian columns. Some parts of the roof and of the architectural elements are beside it.

ΣΟΦΙΑ
ΚΕΛΣΟΥ

THE CELSUS LIBRARY

One of the monumental buildings in Ephesus is the Celsus Library. The library was found in 1904 in a very ruined condition. It was restored by the architect and restorator Dr. F. Hueber during 1972-1978. After Julius Celsus Polemeanus who was the pro-council died in Ephesus at the age of 70, his son Tiberius Aquila had this library made as his father's tomb memorial. It is estimated that this library was finished in 117 years. The grave room is under the apsidida, wall in the library. It can be reached with a narrow road which is behind the north wall. The tomb of Celsus is made of high-quality marble. It is ornamented with a Cupid, girlands and rosettes. When the tomb was found and opened in 1904 it was seen that the skeleton was protected with a lead cover. The rom has two floors. On the first floor there are double columns on a podium which is 21m. high and to which there are nine stairs. Among these there are three richly framed doors which lead to the inside. The one in the middle is like in many antique buildings: wider and higher. On the niches between the walls are four inscripted statues. These represent the virtue (Sophia), science (epusteme), fate (ennoia) and wit (arete) of Celsus. The originals of these statues are in Vienna. During the restorations their copies were made and brought here. The columns on the second floor also have corynthian captions but they are smaller. Their pediments follow this order: one semi-circle, one triangle. Behind the columns above the doors there are three windows. The inner doors of the library have two rows of niches. In front of the first row there is stone scat. In the niches there used to be 12,000 books. To protect these against humidity, the backs of the walls were kept empty. The inside measures of the library are 10.92x16.72 m. Although it seems like it has two floors it only seems so because of the niches. And in front, it is supposed that there was a balcony with a bannister.

Celcius Library and Sophia Statue in Niche (left)

Sophia

Ephisteme

The part above the grave room on the west wall is apsisidal. A statue that was found during the excavation supposedly belongs to Celsus or his son and it is also supposed that the statue used to be in this semi-circular apsis. This staute is being exhibited at the Istanbul Archeological museum.

The library was finished by the heirs because Celsus'es son Tiberius Julius Aquila died before the building was finished. Aquila left 25,000 dinars to obtain the book-rolls. Because the library was made after the buildings around it (the Mazeus Mithrdates Gate on the north, and the altar on the south) some changes in perspective were made to achieve the required monumental appearance. To do so the podium on which columns stand was in a bow-shaped fashion (the middle high and the sides lower). The construction elements such as the columns on both sides and their captions were made smaller in order to make seem farther away than the others.

The wooden construction elements burned down with the Gothic attacks in 262 A.D. but the front wall was not affected very much. In the 4th century this wall was restored together with other buildings and a small fountain was made in the small square in the front. The wall was destroyed in an earthquake in the 10th century.

During the excavations, frizzed blocks which show the Parth wars on both sides of the fountain niches were found. It is estimated that the frizz belonged to the altar on the south of the building. The Marble Road, the stairs which come from the library and the altar altogether give an auditorium-like appearance. The late-period wall and gate in front of the library were built when the city was smallened. The tomb next to the wall was found during an excavation conducted by the museum in 1968: The inscription on it says that it belongs to T. Claudius Flavianus Dionysus. It was made in the 2nd century A.D.

Celcius Library and Mazeus - Mithridates Door

Mazeus - Mithridates Door.

THE MAZEUS-MITHRİDATES GATE AND THE AGORA

The monumental gate next to the library is the south gate of the Ephesus Commerce Agora. Other than this one the Agora has two gates of which one opens up to te Serapis Temple in the west and the other to the Harbor Road. The restoration o these gates has not been started yet. Muzeus ad Mithridates, two slaveş in the services of Emperor Augustus, had this door made because they were set free and they comemorated the gate to Augustus, his wife Livia, his daughter Julia and his son-in-law, Agripa. The gate is in the shape of a victory arch with three passways. Tḥe thick legs between the passways, carry the arch above and also the richly ornamented frizz that is after the arch. At the very top are the attick alls. The passway in the middle is a bit more inward in respect to the others. So the gate obtained a depth and the attickwalls obtained a crown-like appearance.

The dedication inscriptions are on the attick walls of the passways on the sides. On the west:

Im (peratori) caesari Divi f (ilio) Augusto Pontefici

Maximo co (n)s(uli) XII. Tribunic(ia) Podest(ate) xx et

Liviae Caesaris Augusti Mazeus et a livia moglie di Cesare Augusto

M.Agrippae L(ucii) f(ilio) co(n)s(uli) Tert(ium) İmb(eratori) Tribunic(ia)

Podest(ate) vı et Iulia Caesaris Augusti Fil(iae) Mitridates Patronis

The inscription is ın Latin and it is engraved with bronze letters on the atticks. The second line on the east should read "Imp" instead of "imp" but there must have been made a mistake while engraving. The inscription says· "Emperor Caesar, God's son Augustus, the supreme priest, 12 times a council 20 times a tribune and Caesar Augustus'es wife Livia, the son Lucius Marc Agrippa, 3 times a counsil, emperor, 6 times a tribune and the daughter of Caesar Augustus, julia; from Mazeus end Mithridates to their masters and the public." It is estimated that the gate waş built during the 4th and 3rd centuries B.C.

The Agora has a square shape, each side beign 111m. long. Except for the north side on the other sides there are vaulted, small stores. Of these, the ones on the south and east have two floors. Right in front of the stores there are two rows of columns which are covered with a ceiling. The columns are a few steps above the ground. Eventhough the columns were first made of granite, they were replaced with marble ones in the 4th century restorations. Right in the middle there used to beasun and a water clock (horligon). The base of the horligon was found during the excavations.

The Agora was first built in Lysimakhos'es period and found its last shape during Emperor Caracalla's reign (211-217). During the lasets excavations it was seen that the base of the first Agora was 2-3 meters deeper than the present one.

Columns of Agora (up)
General View of Agora (down)

The statuette of Serapis

The plan of Serapis Temple

THE SERAPIS TEMPLE

The staired street on the south-west side of the commerce Agora leads to the Serapis Temple. The main road to the Temple is on the west gate of the Agora. After the gate there is a road 24m. wide and 160m. long and with a stoa appearance. The holy square which seems like a courtyard because of the walls, around it, is connected to this road with a gate. The Temple is placed on a higher terrace on the south end. It has an eight columned prostilos plan. The diameter of each column is 1.5m. and the weight of each is 57 tons. In relation to this all other construction elements are big and heavy as well. The door is wide and has double wings. There are wheels under the door because it is made up of metal and there are holes for the wheels in the doors The construction elements which lie around give the impression that the Serapis Temple was left undone. During the excavations from 1913-1926 a granite statue resembling Egyptian ones was found. An inscription found in the same place tells that this Temple was dedicated to Serapis. In Roman religions there is no life after death. According to the Romans, the dead walk around as souls in the other world. But Egyptian religions promise people to come alive again after death.

All along history, Ephesus was in close relations with Egypt: The Egyptian priest Statue found during the excavations, was made in the 6th century B.C. and brought to Ephesus. Other than this, many small sized Egypt oriented statues were found in various places. Alexandria which was founded in the Nile delta during the Hellenistic period was the Ephesus of the Asia State. Alexandria kept its commercial, cultural and social relations with Ephesus always alive. A concord document exhibited in the Ephesus Museum is a proof that the nagotiaion between Alexandria and Ephesus was made by showing the main Gods as witnesses. On one side of a 1m. long marble block there is the statue of the Artemis of Ephesus and on the other side there is the statue of the main Goddess of Alexandria, Serapis.

So the Serapis Cult found its worshippers in Ephesus and in the 2nd century A.D. during the the period of the Antonius the Serapeion was built.

A View from Marble Street

THE MARBLE ROAD

The holy road that winds around the Pion mountain takes the name 'Marble Road' after it reaches the Celsus Library. It resembles the back of a fish because the middle is higher and the sides are lower. The road is evenly covered with white marble blocks. On the columned side there is a columned portic.The stoa which was made during Emperor Neron's reign (54-68 A.D.) overlooks the Road and the Agora. It is still being restored today. The holes on the roadside of the wall, which show a very fine workmanship were made during the poverty period of Ephesus in order to take the lead and iron holders which held the marble blocks together. On the stoa side of the road there are figures of a Bizantine-era woman head, a heart and foot. These caused a joke which says that these were the ads of the Love House. The gladiator engravings seen on the same row were found in various places and they were put here. The drainage that goes under the road, is uncovered here in order for visitors to see. This part of the drainage belongs to the buildings beneath the Pion mountain and whose excavations have not been started yet. From here coming from the front of the theater it reaches the main drainage at Harbor Road. The Marble Road follows the Theater Gymnasium and the Stadium and reaches the Corresos Gate. According to an inscription, an Ephesusian called Eutropios had some parts of the Road repaired in the 5th century A.D. and the citizens had his statue made. The restorations of the 4th century went as far as the Theater Gymnasium. Because the restorations did not go any further the tracks of the carts which have gone back and forth for centuries, can be seen clearly. The fewness of the tracks on the restored places might indicate that the roads very used very little after the restorations. The arch-piece which was made of eyen bricks and which was found quite undestroyed may indicate that there used to brick walls among the columns and that the gallery was covered with wood.

EY

THE GRAND THEATER

The big theater which is beneath the Pion mountain and which faces the harbor is one of the buildings which has been most effective in the social and the cultural life of Ephesus. Plays, on certain periods of the year, the big meetings of the public parliament called 'Demos' were held here. When gladiator and wild animal fights were popular in the 3rd and 4th centuries, the theater was used as an arena as well. During its history the incident with St. Paul (which is also mentioned in the bible) took place here. When St. Paul came to Ephesus a jeweller named Demetrius who was selling small Artemis statues feared that his statues wouldn't be worth any thing anymore. So he provoked the people and he made them shout: "The Ephesus of Artemis is great, the Ephesus of Artemis is supreme."

The huge theater's most elaborate part is the stage. The inner part of this three-floored section has been made very amazingly and monumentally and a lot of money must have been spent while doing so. The ground floor which has remained unruined until today is made of a narrow corridor which goes from south to north and which has eight rooms on the west side. The door in the very middle of the corridor leads to the orchestra from under the podium. In the classical theaters there were no extra stage constructions. The actors would act in the orchestra section. Together with the hellenistic period, small stages were made for the actors in front of the orchestra. The first stage of the Grand theater was 3m. hide and 3m. high. During the Roman Empire period the width of the stage was increased to 6 meters and the length to 25.5 meters It was again during this period that seats were put in the orchestra part for distinguished audiences. During the reign of Claudius, changes according to the needs of the day were made. The stage was lenthened 3 more meters forwardly but the shape remained the same. Other than that, a wall of three-floored

Views from Grand Theater

columns was put at the back. Its height was 18 meters. The wall was ornamented richly with niches and engravings. In addition the two paradoses were closed and instead narrow entrances in tunnel shapes were made. Of these, the one on the north remained unruined until today but the other one had been closed down earlier. The proscene could be reached through five different doors. The door in the middle is bigger than the others. On its niche above there used to be the statue of the emperor. These changes which started during Claudius'es time lasted for 70 years.

During the play the chorus would enter in one row and take its place on stage and when it was their turn they would recite in unision. The altar which had to be in the middle was used for offering immolations to Dionysus and making ceremonies. This was necessary since

Stage and Remains of the Stage Building

theater was born from Dionysus ceremonies. The hellenistic orchestra of which only very little is left, was much smaller. The diameter was widened 5 more meters during the Roman period. Very few of the ground coverages were found and the present ones were made by imtating these few.

The place where the audience sat, the cavea is 38 meters high and its diameter is 154 meters. In can take, 24,000 people. There were two diazomas,diazomas which made it easier for the audience to take its seat From the orchestra there were 12 stairs which lead to the diazomes. On the sides of some of the stairs there are marble lion heads. The audience would follow the staired row and take their seats. And the doors which were at the top row were used for entrance and exit. These doors would open up to a gallery which was made for better acoustics and to give an orderly look to the cavea. Earlier there used to be bannisters between the cavea and the orchestra but later the present wall was built. The cavea took its last shape with the changes made during the reigns of Emperor Neron and Emperor Septimus Severus.

The plays would start early in the morning and would last until the night. Entrance was charged. Mostly coin shaped tickets made of lead were used. Distinguished people had seats with their names written on them. In very hot weather awning was used to cover some parts. All players were males. They would act various parts by wearing masks. Having watched the same play many times the audience would watch the play knowing its end.

The small, columned building on the side which faces the road is a small fountain. It has two columns with ionic captions and it also has a small pool. The columns would carry the two ceiling casettes which today are beside the fountain. The taps are in the shape of lion heads. The fountain was built in the 2nd century B.C. and was widened with two, carelessly added columns in the 4th century A.D.

Grand Theater - Entrance of the Marble Street.

Harbour Street - Arcadien Road

THE HARBOR ROAD

The 500 meter long road that leads from the Theater to the Harbor is called the Harbor Road. It was made in the 1st century B.C. But it took its last shape with the repairs and restorations during the reign of Emperor Arcadius; thus it is also called the Arcadian. It is 11 meters wide. It was rather used for ceremonial reasons. People coming from overseas would enter Ephesus from this road, and the roads coming from inner Anatolia would end here. So because of this many important people such as emperors and procouncils were welcomed on or sent away from this road. The north side of the road was preserved for sport areas. On the south side there were stores behind a row of covered columns. The walls seen today behind the stores is from the period when Ephesus was growing smaller. At that period the harbor was already filled up and so the street had no importance anymore. And so the road was left out of the boundaries of the city. In an inscription found it says that there used to be fifty street along the road. During the Roman period only very few cities could be lighted. Among these, other than Ephesus, we can count only Rome and Antiokheia. Eventough the road started with the monumental gate in front of the theater and ended with another gate at the harbor, these walls are all destroyed now. The four columns which are in the middle of the road and which were different from the others, supposedly carried statues Their pedestals have remained.

In an inscription found on Harbor road we learn how much money people were charged for formal procedures. According to the inscription the parsley selling was one dinarus, salt one dinarus, being champion in the races six dinarus, salt one dinarus, being champion in the races six dinarus, birth certificate one dinarus, if the person giving birth was Roman then this would cost 100 dinarus.

THE THEATER GYMNASIUM

It is the biggest gymnasium in Ephesus. It is on the north edge of the Road by the theater side. It faces the Harbor road and the Marble Road which goes on after the Theater. No excavation except for its Paleistra (sports area) has been done. The paleistra is on the Harbor side and its measures are 70x70 meters. Its three sides are surrounded by covered columns. The stairs on the south which were used as tribunes also served as entrance to the main building. The gymnasium is symmetrical to the south-north directions. In the south there was the bath with all of its sections, on the sides were classes and conferece rooms. The Emperor Hall was on the north and like in all other gymnasiums apsisidal.

On the north edge of Harbor Road, after the Theater Gymnasium, there was the Verulanus Sports Area. Its measures are 200x240 meters. It was made by the Asia state head priest Verulanus during Emperor Hadrianus'es reign.

THE HARBOR GYMNASIUM AND BATH

After the Verulanus sportsarea there is an ecliptical courtyard. From the gate on the south of the courtyard, which is surrounded by columns and whose floors are covered with mosaic, one can enter the Harbor Gymnasium, the Atrium. On both sides of the gate are two pools which are ornamented with bull heads carrying girlands. The measures of the gymnasium are 40x20 meters and it has two floors. The bronz athlete, the marble child playing with a duck, the Heracles and Kentaurus statues were taken to Vienna. The Harbor Gymnasium was made during Emperor Hadrianus'es period.

A column from Harbour Road

The Hadrianus Bath is a monumental building built between the harbor and the gymnasium. Its measures are 170x160 meters and it is 28 meters high. On the east there is a long hall which takes up the whole of this side. On its left and right there are sections of the bath. The hall which has an ecliptic pool is the frigidarium. The granite columns in the central hall and in other various places, were 11 metres high.

The bath was made in the 2nd century A.D. and restored during the reign of Constantine II (337-361)

Reconstruction of Harbour Door.

THE HARBOR

The wide swamp which starts immediately after Harbor Road is the filled up Harbor of Ephesus. The distance between Ephesus and the Harbor grew wider and wider every year because of the sill carried by the Kaystros River and finally at the end Ephesus completely lost its harbor. Around it are ruins of bonded warehouses and there is also a small lake.

Being built by the seaside was an important factor in the development of Ephesus. After the harbor became non-functional the city became uninhabitable. The citizens who were aware of this fact took many precautions to save the Harbor from the Kaystros River. During the Pergamon Kingdom period, King Attalos II deepened the sea-side part of the harbor and he also built a breakwater so that big ships could come way in, but he could not stop the river. In 61 A.D. the Precouncil by deepening the harbor, Emporor Hadrianus by changing the river bed tried to prevent the filling. Eventhough a wealthy citizen tried to clean up the harbor by spending 20,000 dinariuses all efforts were in vain. Today by the seaside there are walls and breakwaters for sending the river water away. During an excavation made on a small hill, walls for saving the harbor were found.

THE COUNCIL CHURCH (VIRGIN MARY CHURCH)

The Council church which is behind the Harbor baths is one of the most important buildings for Christianity in Ephesus. Other than being the first church having been built for Mary, its importance is that the first council meeting (431 A.D.) which determined the first outlines of Christianity was held here.

The church is next to the Olympeion which is the Emperor Cult Temple and which was represented by Emperor Hadrianus. While the Olympeion was being built there was the Museion instead of the Church. In the Museion medicine and other sciences were taught for higher education. Besides, priests came here to master. In one of the inscriptions found in the building it says that the medicists and professors working at the Museion had tax exemption.

The museion whose walls were made small, even stones, or big blocks, had three esplanades. In the 4th century it was changed into a basilica, being loyal to the original plan. Meanwhile the apsis seen on the east wall, the atrium and baptisterium on the west side were added. The middle esplanade is a bit bigger than the others. Between, were bannisters and columns. Before the atrium there is a nartecs made of mosaic. The floor of the atrium is covered with marble plates which were collected from different parts of Ephesus. Some of these are inscripted but some cannot be read anymore. Under the apsis of the atrium on the west wall is a cistern. The baptisterium has a round shape. It is covered with a cuppola. On the wall are three niches and in the center there is the baptism pool.

During Emperor Justinien's period the basilica again underwent some changes. It was turned into a church with a single cuppola in the middle. Meanwhile for entrance and exit, wide, arched gates to the south and north sides and an exonartecs in front of the nartecs were added.

The big marble cauldron in the middle of the church was brought over from the Harbor Bath during the construction of the last church. In the 10th century a small chapel was built on the south end of the church. The restoration of the church is still being continued by the Ephesus Museum.

During the council meeting in the Virgin Mary church the topic discussed was: "Mary was not the mother of God Christ but she was the mother of human Christ". Nestorius who came up with this idea while he was at the Antiocheia church, defended it more fiercely and tried to spread it after he became the patriarch of Istanbul. When Emperor Theodosius saw that the efforts of spreading these ideas created chaos, he asked for the third general council meeting. 200 clergymen among who were Cyril, the patriarch of Alexandria, Nestorius, the patriarch of Istanbul, John the patriarch of Antiokheia and the representative of the Pope, attended, john, the patriarch of Antiokheia and the representative of the Pope, attended the meeting. The discussion lasted three months. Ephesus went through some dangerous days because of this meeting. The first offical announcement which said that Mary had come to Ephesus and stayed there for a short while, in the house which stood there before the church or somewhere very near and that she was buried in Ephesus, was made during this meeting.

General View of Mary Church

Southern Door of Stadium

THE STADIUM

It is by the north exit on the skirt of the Panayır mountain and it is placed there with the help of the slope. The stadiums where many sports activities took place were inseparable from city life. Boxing, wrestling and running games were held there at certain times.

The entrance to the stadium is through a monumental gate on the west. The pedestals belonging to the two rows of columns of the gate have remained until today. The marble plates decorated with figures of vases and rabbits were brought from other parts of the city and used here.

The seats were made by carving the mountain. The other parts were heightened by vaulted galleries and seats were placed on these. The vaulted galleries are in the form of long corridors.

The Ephesus stadium is the first one made in the Hellenistic period. It got its present shape in the 1st century A.D. by being enlargened. Because gladiator and wild animal fights became very popular in the 3rd and 4th centuries these were held in front of a big number of spectators in stadiums or theaters. Later the stadium has been destroyed by Christians after Christianity became the official religion, because Christians had been massacered there earlier. This is the main reason why none of the seats have remained undestroyed. The marble seats have been for the restoration of the Stadium road and the St. John Church

THE CAVERN OF THE SEVEN SLEEPERS

The asphalt road that goes from the east of the Vedius gymnasium leads to the Cavern of the Seven Sleepers. The most important problem of the christians living in the Roman Empire and who could not get along with state, was the Emperor's cult. If they did not give any sacrifices, which was a necessity of the cult, they were announced the enemy of the state and they were treated as traitors.

In the 3rd century A.D., seven young christian men, because they did not want to give any sacrifices to the Emperor cult, fled from the city and took shelter in the cave, known today as the Cavern of the Seven Sleepers. After they woke up from their sleep and went to town to get some food they realized that they hadn't slept for one night but instead for 209 years and that Christianity was by then wide-spread. When Emperor Theodosius found out about this the took it as a proof of the 'Ressurrection Doctrine'. After the seven young men died they were buried in the cave and a church was built on top of their graves.

In the excavation done in the cave a church and hundreds of graves were found. There are inscriptions for the seven sleepers who are considered holy, on the tombs and on the church walls dated as the 6th century A.D. The desire of being buried as close as possible to the Seven Sleepers has lasted for centuries. According to Christian belief St. Mary Madelaine is buried here.

A column from Artemision (right)

Reconstruction of Artemis Temple

THE ARTEMİS TEMPLE AND THE ARTEMIS CULT

Many Artemis statues have been found during the excavations in Turkey. After these statues have been examined it is now clear that Artemis has gone through an evolution which has lasted for thousands of years. The earliest ones were those found in Çatalhöyük, a district near Konya. These small statues made of soil were fat figures with an exaggerated penis and which represented fertility. Eventhough they were first labelled as Venus it was later understood that this was the earliest mother Goddess of Anatolia. These small statues are dated back to the 7th century B.C. Similar ones dated dated back to the 6th century B.C. were found in Hacılar, a district near Burdur. The mother goddess from there spread first, all over Anatolia, from there to the Balkans and further to Europe, and in the south to Mesopotamia and the Arabic countries. We do not know what the inhabitants of Çatalhöyük and Hacılar called her. The Egyptians have named her Isis, the Arabs named her Lat and the later inhabitants of Anatolia have named her Kubaba, Kybele, Hepa and Artemis. Kybele is the most common among these. In Europe and Anatolia girls are still given this name, although slightly changed. It is understood from the archeological ruins that there used to be Kybele Temples before the Artemis Temples in Ephesus and Sardes.

The most famous Central Anatolian cult center is in Pesinus near Ankara. The Sivrihisar-Ballıhisar köyü. The mother goddess underwent its most important stage of evolution in Pesinus, the capital of Frigya. There she looked like a black meteor in the form of a statue and which had fallen from the sky (a Diopedes). This meteor has been saved in the Kybele Temple and its copies in high-relief have been made on many rocks in Frigya. This statue shaped meteor has been taken to the Kybele Temple on the Platina hill in Rome with a big ceremony so that the Kartaca-Roman war would end in favor of the Romans.

The Goddess has also a Ksonaon appearance. Ksonaon means carved of wood. It is believed that earliest Artemis statues were made of wood. This statue which was carved without many details has been worshipped for many many years.

The oriental side of the Artemis of Ephesus was always more dominant. Strabon says that the priests of the Roman Temple had come from the east. The social structure of the Temple is different from those in the west. Even the terminology was different from the west although greek was the official language. The Artemis Temple was managed by the Headpriest Megabysos. The Headpriest and the other priests were castrated. Around the priests there used to be virgins who were their helpers. It was a great honor to be a priest, especially the headpriest, in the Artemis Temple. There was another class of priests who were called the Currettes, in the Temple as well. These Currettes were half gods who were in good relations with Zeus. While Leto was giving birth to Artemis in Ortygia, they made a lot of noise so that Hera, the real wife of Zeus would not hear the cries of child Artemis. This event was celebrated in a dramatic way every year in Ortygia. Other than the Curettes there used to be another class of priests who were called the Acrobats or The-Ones-Walking-on-Their-Toes. It is supposed that these priests had to do with the dance parts of the ceremonies. Together with these, the number of priests and nuns serving the Temple, reached a few hundreads.

Another social activity of the Temple was that it also used to function like a bank. It was the duty of the Headpriest Megabysos to accept entrusted valuable belongings and to give credit from the Temple budget.

The Asyl right which was given only very rarely to Temples was given to the Ephesus Artemis temple. If anybody took shelter after committing a crime he had the right to stay for a long time in the Temple. The sacred area of the Temple went through changes from time to time. While the Asyl timits used to be very narrow until Alexander they were enlargened during his period. Later King Mithridates largened even these limits. Emperor Marcus Antonius enlargened it twice as much after Julius Caesar did the same thing to Dydima. So this privileged area started to include some parts of the city. Because the asyl limits were enlargened, too many criminals started to gather in the Temple. This started a series of complaints because the same thing happened in other parts of the Empire. The lifting of the asyl right came into question many times. In the year 22 A.D. Emperor Tiberius called for the representatives of the famous Temples to discuss the matter. But the asyl right of the Artemis Temple was not lifted.

Strabon says that the Temple was torn down and rebuilt seven times the Temple which used to be right by the seaside, during antiquity, is now 5 kms away because of the alluvions brought by the Kaystros River. Only four stages could have been brought about with the excavations. The earliest pieces found in the Temple were ceramic bowls with geometrical designs on them. These bowls which are estimated to be made in the 7th century B.C. are as old as the first Temple. It is supposed that this Temple was torn down by the Kimmers. In the years 560-550 B.C. the largest Temple in Ionic style with a dipteros plan a with the measures of 115-55.10 meters was built. According to Plynius the 127 columns of the Temple resembled a forest. The columns were 19 meters high. The 36 columns in the front had high-reliefs on them. These reliefed drums were first thought on the column pedestal but it has been concluded that they must have been right under the column frontals. The architects of this Temple were Theodoros from Samos and Chersiphron of Knossos on his son Metagenes. The reason why Theodoros was called from Samos as an architect was that this Temple had to resemble the Hera Temple in Samos and also because the ground was swampy just like the Heraion. Theodoros used the same technic as in the Temple of Hera: one layer of coal and one layer leather. It is obvious that Chersiphron of Crete and his son must have known the architectures of Egypt and Hitite very well. The Columna Caelatar has been made by Croises and he gave it as a present to the Temple.

The archaic Artemis Temple was burnt down on the night the Great Alexander was born (July/23/356), by someone called Herostratos because he wanted to immortalize his name. The reliefed column with the name of Croisos on it and other valuable Temple present such as gold and ivory were found during excavations and taken to the British Museum.

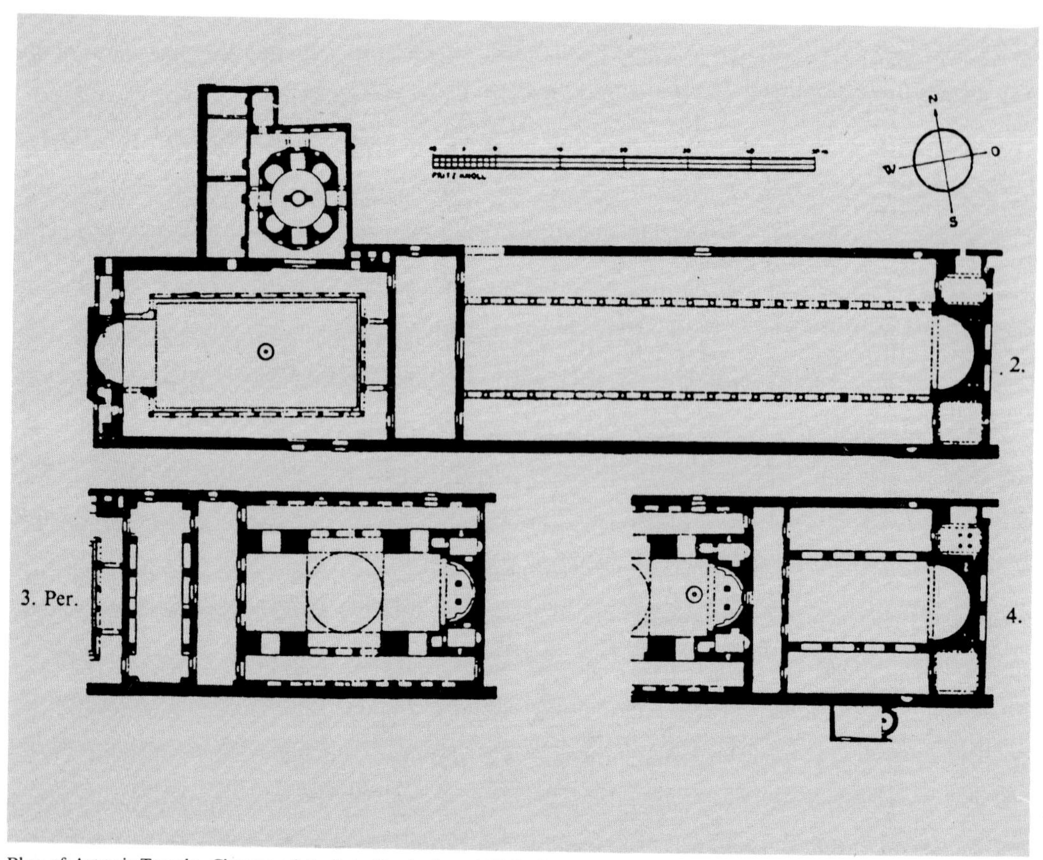

Plan of Artemis Temple, Changes of Archaic Era (up), and Hellenistic Era (down)

After the Temple was burnt down the citizens started to work on a more elaborate Temple. Eventhough they stayed quite loyal to the archaic plan the podium was heightened 2.68 meters and 13 stairs (krepis) were built around it. Its length was 105 and its hieght 55 meters. The former plan and shape were the same, the columns in the front were in high relief just like in the former Temple. According to the information given by Plinius and Vitrivius, one of the columns was made by the famos sculptures, Scopas. It is also said that Praksiteles himself had worked on the altar in front of the Temple.

The altar being in the shape of a cornered "U", took place in front of the Temple with 92 long, thin ionic columns which were in two rows. In the two inner corners there were four cart (quadriga) statues. One of the horses is being exhibited at the Ephesus Museum. On one of the columns, which is at the British Museum, there is the tragic story of Alkestis who is taken to be slain because he has agreed to sacrifice his life in order to save that of his wife.

In the 5th century B.C. a competition among the most famos sculptures of the time was made because of the Amazon Statue which was going to be put in the Artemis Temple. According to Plinius Phedias, Polykleitos, Kresilas and Phradmon took place in the compet ition. After the statues were finished, it was left up to the sculptures to choose the winner. During the voting each artist voted best for his piece and second best for that of Polykleitos. So Polykleitos won because he had the most number of votes and his statue obtained the right to be put into the Temple. Today there are only copites of these Roman Era statues and it is not definite which one belongs to Polykleitos.

The Artemis Statue - 1. st. C.B.C.

View of St. John Church (up) and its plan (down)

THE ST.JOHN CHURCH

After the apostles were throcon out of Jerusalem St. John came to Ephesus together with Virgin Mary. He took charge of the Ephesus church after St.Paul had been killed in Rome, and he tried to spread christianity. After his death he was buried on the south side of the hill where the Seljuk castle in and afterwards a basilica was built on his grave. During the reign of Justinien, a church, of which we can still see the ruins, was built inplace of the basilica. After the Arabic attacks became to get effective in the 7th century, the church was included to the castle on top of the hill, by the walls which were built around it According to Ibn-i Batuda the church was used as a mosque in the beginning of the 14th century. The church lost its importance completely when in 1375 the Isabey Mosque was built between the chruch and the Artemis Temple.

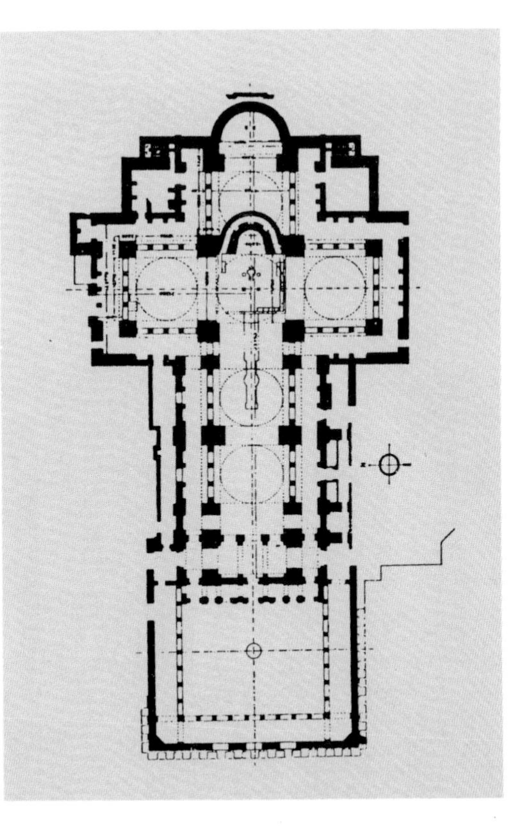

Main Entrance of Basilica (Pursuit Door) (up)
Views from St. John Church

The entrance of the St. John church is through the Takip Gate on the south. Other than this the church has two other gates which open up to the to the West and East. Of those the one facing west and which leads to the Isabey mosque has been excavated and it restorations have been finished.

The Takip gate is protected by two, high and thick towers. Inside there is a courtyard. The marble construction materials which have been used to build the courtyard and the towers, were brought over from other buildings of Ephesus. The inscriptions seen in the courtyard were found in Various places during the excavation of the church. The marble covered road after the courtyard leads all the way to the church. The road parallel to this and which has a side walk was made during the reign of the Seljuk Terks.

The St. John church can be studied, from the west, in these parts: The atrium the narteks, the esplanade and side constructions.

The atrium is 35m. long and 47m. wide and it is on the west end of the church. The middle is an empty square surrounded by a gallery made of columns.

On the east of the atrium is the natreks in the shape of a narrow corridor. Through the narteks which has five cuppolas, you can enter the main part with three doors each covered with an esplanade. The main part has three esplades and is cross shaped. The center esplanade is wider than the others. It was covered with six cuppolas. The side esplanades were covered with vaults. The cuppolas are completely ruined today. They were carried by the thick legs made of bricks and marble. Among the legs were Bizantine style columns, white and with blue veins. In the center of the column captions which face the esplanade are the monograms of justinien and his wife Theodora. The archs used to carry the second floor columns. The grave of St. John is in the room in front of the apsis and which is lower than the ground floor. All The mosaics have been taken by visitors from the middle ages up until now, and so the ones seen today were made later. The thin columns in the grave room used to carry the cuppola there. The belief that there used to rise healing dust from the window by the columns caused many ill people to visit the church.

Fountain Building

The building seen next to the grave and which is covered with tiles, is a chapel built in the 10th century. In its apsis are the frescos of Jesus Christ St. John and an unknown saint. One end of the corridor which is in front of the chapel, leads to the skevophlakion (the treasury) and the other end leads to the baptisterium. Both of these are round in shape and they have cuppolas. The treasure room has two floors. The baptisterium pool has remained in good shape until today. The fountain which stands between the baptisterium and the esplanade and which has a frontal and a pool used to be a grave but it was later turned into a fountain.

The interior of Virgin Mary House

THE VIRGIN MARY HOUSE

The road which starts immediately after the Magnesia gate and winds toward Bülbül Mountain leads all the way to Virgin Mary's house. This house which is placed at the beginning of a steep valley is known as the place where Mary spent her last days.

According to the Bible of St. John, Jesus entrusted Mary to St. John before he was crusified. The histographer Eusebios says that the Asia state witnessed many activities of St. John during 37-42 after the apostles were thrown out of Jerusalem. It would be impossible to imagine that St. John would leave Mary behind while there was still chaos in Jerusalem. According to council records, Mary, for a very short time, lived in a house near the council church and then she moved to her house on Bülbül Mountain where she lived for 46 years. She died in Ephesus when she was 64 years old. The house was slowly forgotten because Christianity was not so much widespread at those times.

A german lady called Anna Katerina Emmerick (1774-1824) who lived in the town of Dülmen in the Westfalen region who physically was unable to walk, who had never left her bed nor her town and had never visited any other place wrote a book under the name 'The Life of Mary' and together with many revelations she describes the house and its place. A priest called Gouyet who was committed to the Parisian Bishopric wen to Ephesus to check out the revelations. The headbishop of Izmir, Timoni helped him very much. Eventhough Gouyet claimedhe found the house nobody believed him. Ten years after this, the Lazarien priest jung startedan expendition under the support of Eugene Pouline, the headmaster of the French high-school of Izmir. Later on Pouline personally attended the expedition and the trueness of A.Katerina Emmerik's revelations was thereby proven. Later in 1967 Pope Paul VI and in 1979 Pope John II came here to pray and thus made the whole world accept the house of Virgin Mary.

The house has the shape of a crucifix and resembles a small church. The house on the right side of the apsis has been completely destroyed. The small room across this one is known as the bedroom of Mary. The place in front of the apsis covered with black marbles used to be the kichen of the house. By examining the things there it has been understood that the stove was used during the times of Mary. By examining the foundation and the house which is not much higher than the foundation its history back until to the 1st century was figured out. The present walls and the roof were added later. If one takes a close look he can see that there is a thin, red line between the original and the new walls.

The statue seen in Mary's house has been put there later. The big pool seen on the road before reaching the house used to be a big cistern which was made during later periods.

During the excavation which was made on the arched wall by the mountain side, a grave was found under each arch and it was also noticed that the bodies were faced toward the House. There is also a holy fountain on the terrace which is situated in front of terrace of the House.

The exterior of Virgin Mary House (up)
Statue of Virgin Mary (down)

EFES MÜZESİ

THE EPHESUS MUSEUM

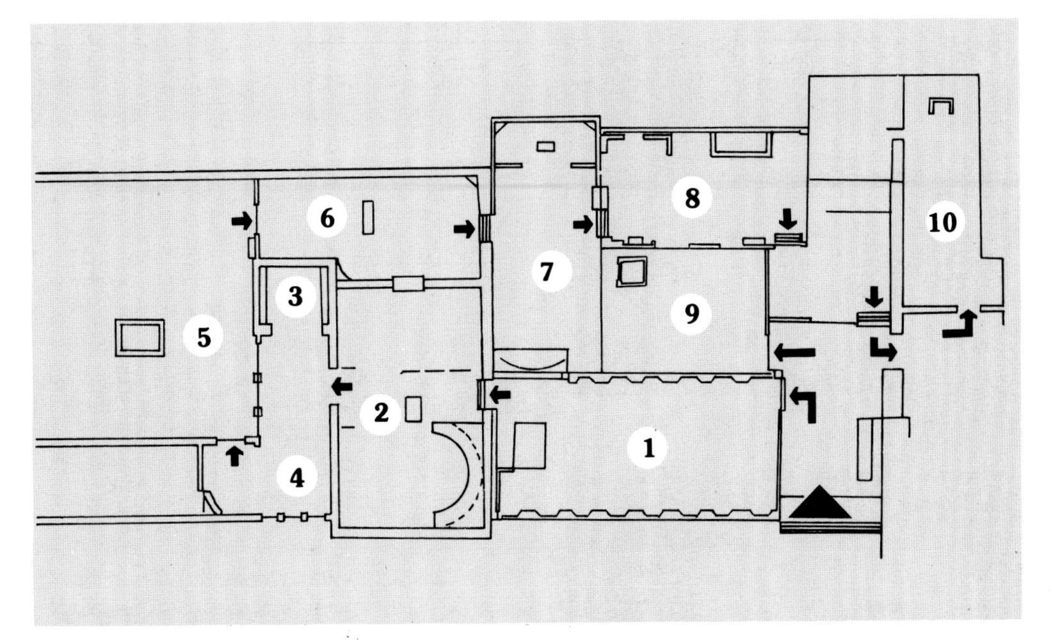

Plan of the Ephesus Museum

1) The House Findings Hall
2) Fountain Findings Hall
3) The New Findings Hall
4) Coins and Treasury Section
5) The Museum Garden
6) Grave Findings Hall
7) The Artemis Hall
8) The Emperors Cult Hall
9) The Courtyard
10) Art Gallery

The Ephesus museum which was built as a warehouse in 1929, is now fulfilling the expectations of the visitors with new additions every year. The 25000 archeologically different pieces which are in the museum were all found in Ephesus. Only about 1000 of these can be exhibited.

These pieces are exhibited according to where they were found instead of chronological order.

Entrance of Ephesus Museum (left)

Arcaisan Artemis Statue 2nd C. A.D.
Priaphos with Tray 2nd C. A.D.

THE HOUSE FINDINGS HALL

The excavations of some of the houses on the hill across the Hadrianus Temple have been completed and the small pieces found are exhibited in this hall. The houses collapsed during the earthquake at the end of the 6th cent. Later, the citizens dug out their most important belongings from under the ground This is why the number of the finidings is so small.

Among the exhibited pieces are marble statues and busts which are 30-70 cms high. The archaic Artemis statue at the entrance of the hall is one of these. As in all archaic period statues, Artemis is standing still and in one hand she is holding an arrow and in the other a bow. Beneath her feet there is a quiver. Next to this one is the statue of Asklepios wrapped up in a cloth that leaves half of his chest bare and in one of his hands he is holding his holy scepter. In the other corner of the room are various busts and statues which are holding opened jewellry boxes and there are smaller heads of statues. Among these the Priapos statue that is holding a fruit tray on his phalios and the Priapos or Bes statue made of ceramic with a huge phallos, are very famous pieces of the Ephesus Museum. The cupid head, made of white marble and which was found at the same time is a copy of the work of the famos sculpture Lissippos which he made during the Roman Empire Era. There is also the bust of the famos comedian Menander and a cupid statue with a rabbitt. The statue shows Cupid holding the rabbitt in his hand and trying to save it from the dog which is by his feet and which is leaning towards the rabbitt.

The bronze statue of Cupid on the back of a dolphin was used as the tap of the fountain or pool of the houses. The water used to run from the eyes of the Dolphin. The table behind the glass is portable. It can be hightened if necessary. Above its legs there are boxer figures of marble and the wooden holders of the table.

Egyptian Monk Statue. Bronze 6th C.B.C.

Statue of Hunter Artemis 1st C. B.C.

Eros and Dolphin. Bronze

In another window in the same row there are wine cups, oil lamps in different shapes, ivory knife handles and bracelets. The bronze egyptian priest statue which is in a small window is the oldest piece in the hall and it is dated back to the 6th century B.C. On the back of the priest there is a hieroglyph inscription. This piece is one of the pieces which has been brought over as a result of the trade between Ephesus and Egypt.

On the panel next to the priest there is a fresco-wall of one of the slope houses of Ephesus. One of the frescos as can be read in the inscripton is Socrates. The other one belongs to a muse. The statue at the wall in the niche is Artemis.

Torso of Aphrodit 1st C. B.C.
Zeus Head 1st C. A.D.

THE FOUNTAIN FINDINGS HALL

The high reliefs and statues of the memorial fountains of Ephesus are being exhibited here. The first piece in the entrance of the hall is a Zeus head from the Hellenistic period. The torso of which the feet and head are missing is Aphrodites with perfect measures. This one also belongs to the Hellenistic period. The statue in the lying position is resting warrior. The warrior who was placed in the triangular frontal of a building is leaning on his turbot and thus half-lying.

The group of statues seen on a circular pedestal was first ornamenting the frontal of the Temple in the middle of the State Agora. Later it was taken next to the pool of the Pollio fountain. The statue which is taking place in the middle of the group and whose head and knee are left only, is Polyphemos, the son of Poseidon. The statue on his right and which is serving him a drink is Odysseus. The ones lying in the front are the ones killed by Polyphemos and the ones on the right end are the friends of Odysseus who get prepared to take out the eyes of Polyphemos after he gets drunk.

The statues found across the Polyphemos group have been found by the Traian fountain. In the drawing above,the positions of the statues have been explained. The statue on the left which resembles an athlete is young Dionysus. Next to him is a naked satyr which used to be at the second floor of the fountain. The other statues belong to the family of the Emperor. The statue in front of the drawing and beside which there is a dog is the founder of Ephesus, Androclos. Next to this one there is another Aphrodites, showing her half-dressed and with an oyster on her stomach. Other pieces exhibited in the hall are the findings of the G.Laeceanus Bassus Fountain. Among these the ones whose clothes seem to be transparent are nymphes and the one on the right the Ephesusian Hera and the ones on the left are tritons. The heads of the statues were made in the Hellenistic and Roman eras and have been in various places in Ephesus.

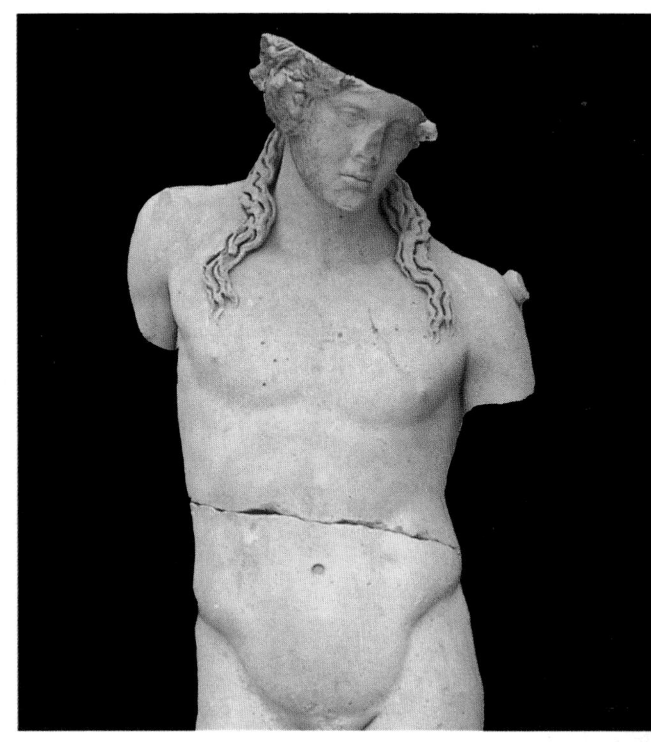

Hera Statue 1st C. A.D.
Aphrodit Statue 50-100 A.D.

Dionysos Statue 2ndC. A.D.
Resting Warrior 1st C. A.D.

Silver Coin 1st C. A.D.
Mask for Tragedy 2nd C A.D.

THE NEW FINDINGS HALL

One can pass to the New Findings Hall through the Fountain Findings Hall. In the first window on the right there are crosses and relics which were found during the St. John excavations and there also are other Bizantian findings. In the west part of the room in the wall windows there are coins which have been found in Ephesus. In the drawing on the wall, the process of making a coin has been tried to explain. The enlargened coin copies at the very top, are actually in the first window on the right. On one of these it says 'The Artemis of Ephesus' and around it, it says 'Diana Ephesia'. On another coin there is a bee which is the symbol of Ephesus and around it are the first two letters of the word Ephesus. Among the treasures exhibited in the right window, there are silver coins which are co-printed by Ephesus, Pergamon and Tralles and thus valid in all three cities. The treasures on the side, in the same window have been found during the St. John excavations in a ceramic piggy bank-like pot. Among these the silver ones are automman and the golden ones are Venecian and they have been made in the 14th century.

The blue glass plate in the window on the left is dated back to the first century. The plate was found in pieces in one of the slope houses and was laer put together. The missing pieces have been completed with polyester. In other windows in the same row there also are wine cups, the bronze snake which was regarded as the protector of the house, the cupid with the dolphin and cupids which are holding masks. On one side of the wall across, there are drama masks and on the other side there are oil-lamps made during various periods of Ephesus.

The bust which is on the east wall of the hall, and which has been preserved in very good shape belongs to Emperor Marcus Aurelius. The ivory frizz on the same side of the wall is one of the most important pieces of the Ephesus Museum. The frizz describes the story of Emperor Traian fighting against the Orientals and it also describes the post war periods.

The Ivory Frieze, 2 nd.c. A.D.
The frieze which has been used as a furniture wall decoration, shows Emperor Traian's war to Easterns.

THE MUSEUM GARDEN

Graves, frontals, inscriptions and are being exhibited in the garden.

The triangular frontal seen in the of the garden is an arrangement which shows the original position of the Polyphemos group which is now in the Fountain Findings Hall and which originally used to be in the Temple in the State Agora. The group used to be in that manner before it was brought to the Pollio fountain.

Among the column captions which are being exhibited under the frontal, the oldest ones are the Artemision Findings and they are dated back to the 6th century A.D. The sun-clock found in the middle of the garden has been made during Emp. Caracalla's reign. The grave with the muse which is next to the was found near the Vedius Gymnasium. The grave on the other side is the famous Belevi memorial grave. The grave which was made like the Halicarnassos Mausoleum in 150 A.D. and which is on the road to Izmir is 15 kms away from Ephesus. The big inscription near the memorial is about harbor laws.

Sarcophagus with Muse 3rd C. A.D.
Project Pediment of Issis or Augustus Temple (down)

A Mycenaean Crater - Terra Cotta approx. 1400 - 1375 B.C.

GRAVE FINDINGS HALL

On the wall panel which is placed on the right entrance wall of the garden side there are descriptive drawings and also explanations about the various important types of graves found in Turkey. Right opposite this wall there is a wall window, in which the most ancient findings, the Micenean cups, are exhibited. These cups which are dated back to the 13-14th centuries B.C. are the most well known pieces of Micenean art. These are ornamented with red sea plants and octopusses and parallel lines on a beige colored surface. In the window next to this one cups which were put in graves that were uncovered by chance were found.

The ceramic grave exhibited in the middle of the hall was made in the 6th century A.D. and it was found in the Ephesus Trade Agora. Because many similar one to this were made in Klozomenai, a district near Çeşme, these graves take the same name. The coins and presents seen in the grave belong to the same period.

The ostotecs exhibited in the right corner of the hall were found in the cavern of the Seven Sleepers. In the miniatures of the wall the Seven Sleepers were described according to Moslem and Christian belief.

As of yet, a glass workshop has not been found during the excavations in Ephesus. But it is known that glass was produced quite a lot like in any other Anatolian city. The pieces of glass found in the graves which were uncovered by chance show that the Roman era glassware was of many different kinds.

On the right wall of the hall we can see the Kybele high-reliefs. Beside the Kybele Statue which was made in a niche in the 5th century B.C., are two lions. On the high-reliefs on the sides there is Kybele in the middle, on one side of her is her priest Attis and her other side there is a Zeus figure. The writings and drawings on the high-relief explain the evolution of Kybele before she turned into Artemis.

Marble Ostotec 2nd C. A.D. (up) Tomb Steles (down)

Grand Artemis Statue

Be'le Artemis Statue 2nd C. A.D.

THE ARTEMIS HALL

The pieces found in the Artemis Temple are being exhibited in this hall. And other pieces concerning Artemis and which were found in different spots of Ephesus are also being exhibited here. The statue which is placed the left side of the entrance is called the Collossal Artemis and it was found in the Ephesus Prythaneion. This Artemis Statue which is the most famous piece of the Ephesus museum carries a pollos made of three storeyed temples on her head. Her eyes are big and it seems as if they look somewhere far away. She is wearing rows of necklaces and there are many lumps on her chest. Although these were first thought to be her breasts it was later realized that these were bull testises. The most obvious implication that she is Kybele are the lions in her arms. Her legs are tightly together as if they were welded. Her skirt is divided both vertically and diagonally and in each piece there is either a bull, a lion, a deer, a sphenx or a griffin. On the sides of her skirt there are also bees which are the symbols of Ephesus. Artemis is holding her arms out as if she were giving out fertility.

The collossal Artemis Statue has been copied in the 1st century B.C. being very faithful to its original examples. Her appearance is totally ksonaon, in other words carved of wood. It is known that the earliest Artemis statue which is in Panionion, the religious center of Ionia, was carved carelessly out of palm or date trees.

The beautiful Artemis which is opposite the Collossal Artemis was found in the same place. The marble of this statue is of higher quality and it is whiter. Her pollos is missing. Beneath her feet are bee baskets and deers. The animals in her skirt are just like the former one. As a difference from the former one there is a zodiac around her neck and this represents her reign over the skies. Some left over gild on the statue gives us a hint in that the statue might have been completely gilded earlier. The small Artemis statue next to this one shows the characteristics as the other ones. It is supposed that the hands and wrists are made of ivory.

In the wall window many presents which were given to the Temple are being exhibited. Among these the gold and ivory statues are head-priest Megabysos. The bronze griffin heads were sometimes used with handles. Most of the pieces in the window were made in the 7th century B.C.

Nun figurine, Gold - 6. th. c. B.C.

Nun figurine, Ivory - 6. th. c. B.C.

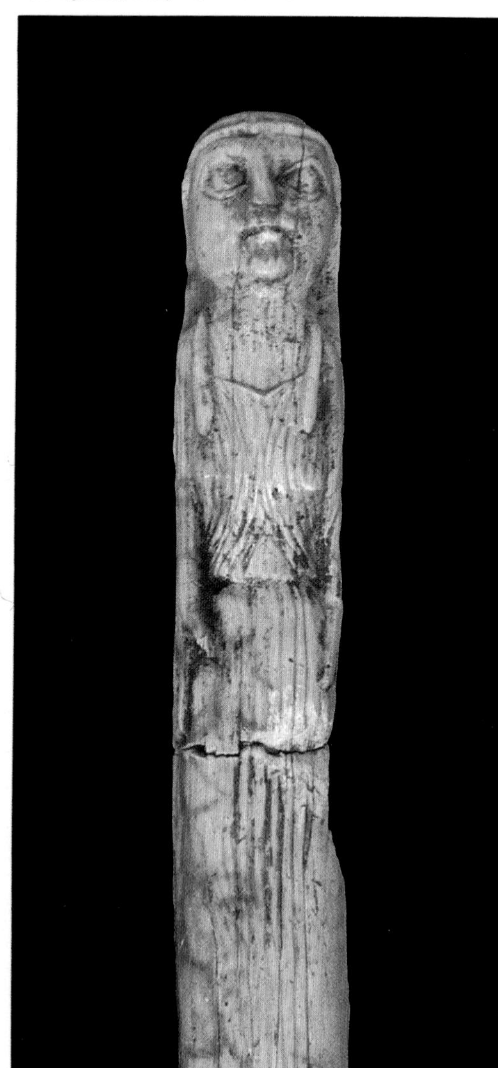

Head of a Man - 3 rd. c. B.C.

Head of a Man - 3 rd. c. B.C.

Head of Traian - 98-117 A.D.

THE EMPEROR'S CULT HALL

The big statue on the left entrance of the wall, and which is still in good shape belongs to counsil Stephan. Stephan was the governor of the Asia State in the name of the Roman Empire in the 4th century A.D. He is holding his hand up and in his hand there is a handkerchief. He is probably about to start a gladiator fight or any other race. The Emperor Hadrian frizze which is opposite the statue has been brought here and copies were put in the original place. On the narrow side there is a bull which is about to be immolated oblated and on the wide side there are weapons and armours, all in high relief. The two statues by the exit door belong to Emperor Augustus and his wife Livia. Both statues were destroyed in the early Christianity era and crucifixes were put on their foreheads.

Head of a Woman

Head of a Woman

The Buste of Augustus - 1. st. c. A.D.

The Buste of Livia - 1. st. c. A.D.

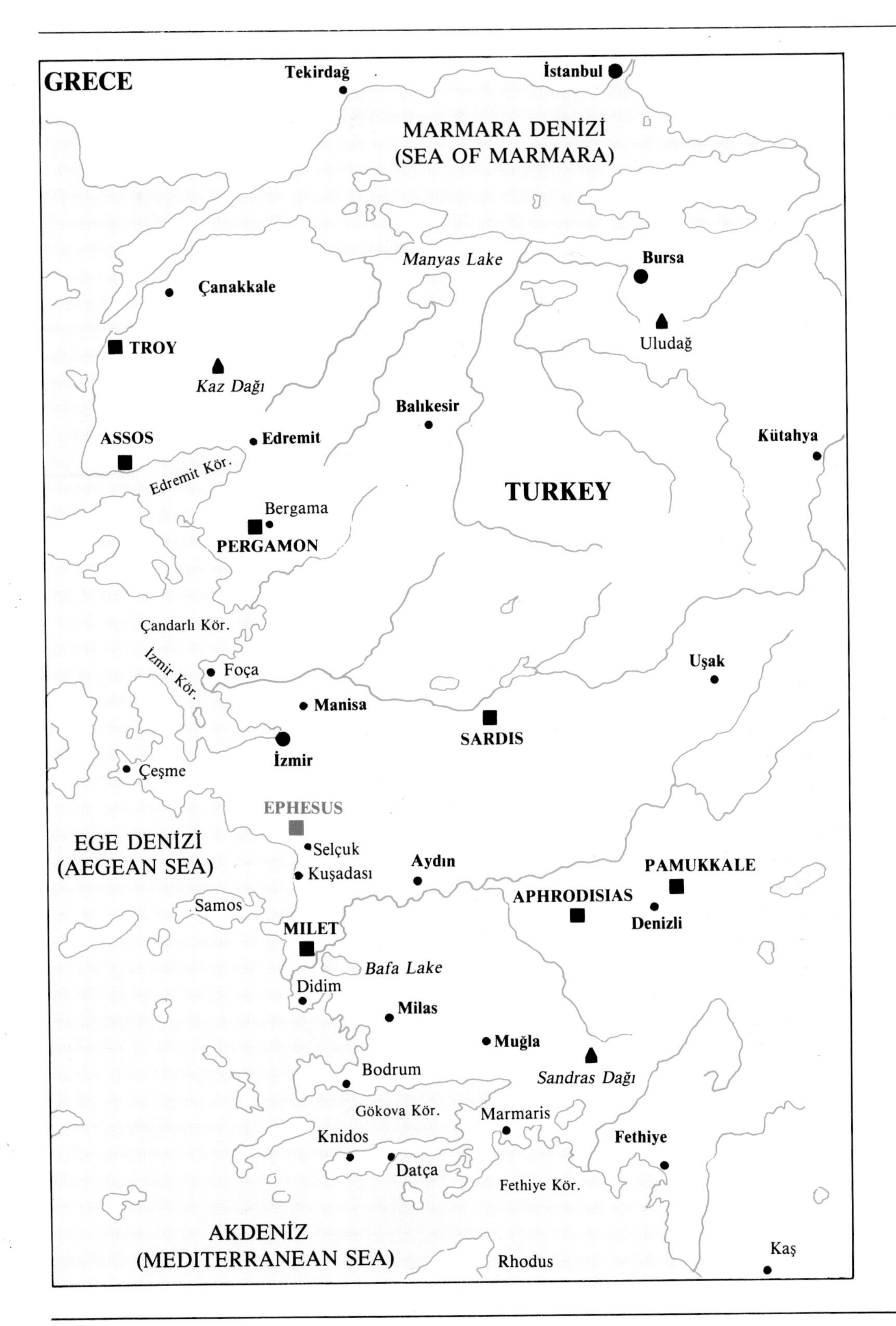
GRECE
Tekirdağ
İstanbul
MARMARA DENİZİ
(SEA OF MARMARA)
Manyas Lake
Bursa
Çanakkale
Uludağ
TROY
Kaz Dağı
Balıkesir
ASSOS
Edremit
Kütahya
Edremit Kör.
TURKEY
Bergama
PERGAMON
Çandarlı Kör.
İzmir Kör.
Foça
Uşak
Manisa
SARDIS
İzmir
Çeşme
EPHESUS
EGE DENİZİ
(AEGEAN SEA)
Selçuk
Kuşadası
Aydın
PAMUKKALE
APHRODISIAS
Denizli
Samos
MILET
Bafa Lake
Didim
Milas
Muğla
Bodrum
Sandras Dağı
Gökova Kör.
Marmaris
Knidos
Fethiye
Datça
Fethiye Kör.
AKDENİZ
(MEDITERRANEAN SEA)
Rhodus
Kaş

BIBLIOGRAPHY

AKURGAL, E.Anadolu Uygarlıkları. İstanbul 1988
AKURGAL, E.Ancient Civilisation und Ruins of Turkey. İstanbul 1985
AKŞİT, İ.Ephesos. İstanbul 1988
BAMMER, A.Die Architektur des Jüngeren Artemision von Ephesos. Wiesbaden 1972
BOYSAL, Y.Grek Klasik Heykeltraşlığı. Ankara 1967
BEAN, G.E. Aegean Turkey. London 1966
COOK, R.M. The Greeks in Ionia and The East. 1962
DUYURAN, R.Efesos Kılavuzu. İstanbul 1972
ERDEMGİL, S.Efes. İstanbul 1986
ERHAT, A.Mitoloji Sözlüğü. İstanbul 1972
EFES MÜZESİ ARKEOLOGLARI. Efes Yamaç Evler. İstanbul 1987
HERODOTOS. Herodot Tarihi. Çev.M.Ökmen. İstanbul 1973
LESSING, E.Ephesos Welstadt der Antike. Wien 1978
MANSEL, A.M. Ege ve Yunan Tarihi. Ankara 1966
MILTNER, F.Ephesos, Stadt der Artemis und des Johannes. Wien 1958
ÖNEN, Ü.Ephese, Ruin et Musee. İzmir 1983
SEVAL, M.Ephesus. İzmir 1988
TÜRKOĞLU, S.ATALAY, E.Efes. İzmir 1978

Eros Head
(2nd. c. A.D)
VARIUS
BATH
ODEON
DEA_ROMA
BASILICA
ISIS TEMPLE
STATE
AGORA
POLLIO
FOUNTAIN
Resting Warrior
(2nd. c. A.D.)
DOMITIAN PLACE
DOMITIAN
TEMPLE
BÜLBÜL MOUNT.
(358m.)
© 1989 MELEK ÖNDÜN

MI 5

BY THE SAME AUTHOR

(with Richard Deacon)
Spy!